THE ILLUSTRATED GUIDE TO
EGYPTIAN
MYTHOLOGY

THE ILLUSTRATED GUIDE TO
EGYPTIAN MYTHOLOGY

LEWIS SPENCE
Introduced by
JAMES PUTNAM

STUDIO

Hieroglyphics (page 1) carved in relief. The oval shapes (cartouches) generally enclose names.

Son-et-lumière at Philae (frontispiece). Begun during the reign of the Ptolemies and completed in Roman times, the temple complex on the island of Philae in Upper Egypt was a major late centre for the cult of Isis and Osiris.

Panorama of modern Cairo (above), with the pyramids of Kheops (Khufu) and Khephren in the background. The modern city has expanded to encompass many sites of historical and mythological importance, including Giza, Memphis and Heliopolis.

First published in 1996 by Studio, an imprint of Random House UK Ltd, 20 Vauxhall Bridge Road, London SW1V 2SA.

Copyright © 1996 Studio. Reprinted 1997.

ISBN 1 85891 425 6

Picture research by Julia Hanson
Text compilation and captions by Simon Hall
Designed by Rachel Griffin, Ray Shell Design

Printed and bound by Oriental Press (Dubai)

Publisher's Note
The names of Egyptian gods, goddesses and places appear as they were written in Lewis Spence's original classic text of 1915 and may not necessarily correspond with modern spellings.

CONTENTS

INTRODUCTION

By James Putnam

Egypt has one of the oldest civilizations in the world, which as far back as five thousand years ago had developed a style of writing, great towns, impressive monuments and a strong centralized monarchy under the pharaoh. Just how enduring their culture was can best be expressed by considering that over two-and-a-half thousand years separate the building of the pyramids from the reign of Queen Cleopatra. To the pharaoh Tutankhamun, whose brief reign falls around the middle of this entire period, these pyramids were already ancient history! However, this extraordinary civilization did not just arrive in the Nile Valley out of nowhere; it took time to develop, and had its own stone age which produced beautiful pottery and flint knives. This late Neolithic period in Egypt, which dates back beyond 5000 BC, is called Predynastic as a precursor to pharaonic Egypt with its dynasties of Kings. By convention Egyptologists divide this part of history into thirty dynasties, after a system devised by Manetho, an Egyptian priest living in the Greek era, about 300 BC. It is also convenient to break down the long history into three main periods called the Old Kingdom (c.2613–2160 BC), the Middle Kingdom (c.2040–1750 BC) and the New Kingdom (c.1550–1086 BC). There were intervals or dark ages between these Kingdoms – the so-called intermediate periods – when governments were weak, or there was civil war or foreign invasion. The Egyptians themselves recorded the names of rulers and the length and order of their reigns, and two important surviving texts are the Turin Royal Papyrus and the British Museum stone King List. They also recorded major astronomical events, which we are able to date ourselves fairly exactly and thus verify Egyptian chronology.

Environmental conditions and, in particular, the agricultural dependence on the River Nile were vital to Egypt's development as a great civilization. The Ancient Greek historian Herodotus appropriately referred to Egypt as "the gift of the Nile" since without it the country would be largely desert. The Nile is the longest river in the world and flows in total for over four thousand miles. Only along its banks could this agricultural

A granite colossus of Ramesses II (opposite), the most powerful of the Egyptian pharaohs of the New Kingdom, at Karnak. Before him stands the figure of a queen, possibly his daughter.

7

Elaborate interior of Tutankhamun's tomb, discovered in 1922, in the Valley of Kings near Luxor.

nation survive in a country of almost zero annual rainfall. The Ancient Egyptians called their land Kemet, "the Black Land", because of the rich black silt that the Nile deposited on its banks after the annual flood. This was caused by the increased rainfall far away in the heights of Ethiopia. Careful irrigation enabled the Egyptians to produce vast amounts of crops, but if the flood failed there was disastrous famine. A nation-wide organization of resources was therefore necessary; reserves of grain were stored as a precaution against famine and there was a strict system of national service and taxation. During the flood season of the Nile, a vast workforce of agricultural labourers unable to farm the land became available for maintaining the irrigation channels and working on large building projects such as the pyramids and the temples.

The Egyptians named the desert Deshret, "the Red Land", and the contrast with the fertile "Black Land" aptly symbolized the juxtaposition of life and death. Reflected in nature they saw the perpetual cycle of life, death and rebirth which had an inseparable connection to their religious beliefs.

The country divides naturally into Lower Egypt, the fertile Delta region northwards from the ancient capital Memphis, near modern Cairo, and Upper Egypt, the southern-most part of the country, which extends along the narrow valley to Aswan. The history of dynastic Egypt was traditionally born with the conquest of the north by a southern king, called Menes, who proceeded to make himself king of a united Egypt. Egyptologists now believe that the process of unification was not the outcome of a single battle, but was a gradual process that took over two hundred years. A famous ceremonial palette survives which is thought to depict just such a triumph by the victorious King Narmer, over a northern enemy. On one side he is shown wearing the White Crown of Upper Egypt and on the other side he appears in the Red Crown of the Lower Egyptian king whose rule extended over the Delta and beyond. Every succeeding pharaoh proclaimed himself in his title as being "King of Upper and Lower Egypt". He was also called "Son of the Ra", the sun god, and was regarded by his subjects as both god and king, and therefore worthy of labour on building projects of super-human scale.

Crops in Egypt's almost rainless climate have always depended on good irrigation. Here a traditional bullock-powered pump lifts Nile water.

An illustration of Pharoah Narmer, traditionally the uniter of Upper and Lower Egypt at the beginning of the Old Kingdom, executing a prisoner of war, from a British Museum original.

The Old Kingdom saw the establishment of a powerful state, and in about 2680 BC King Djoser's architect Imhotep designed, for his pharaoh's tomb, the Step Pyramid at Saqqara, which is the earliest large stone building in the world. About a hundred years later, the kings were buried in 'true' pyramids and the three at Giza, built for Khufu, Khafre and Menkaura represent the peak of building achievement. They are the only one of the Seven Wonders of the Ancient World still standing, and at 481ft (146m) the Great Pyramid was the tallest building on earth until the Eiffel Tower was erected in 1889. By the end of the Old Kingdom the pyramids were smaller and their construction was of a lower standard, and Egypt itself fell into a state of rapid decline. Recovery came with the reign of King Mentuhotep I, who ruled a united kingdom again in about 2000 BC. He consolidated Egypt's borders, pacified the land with his military activities and restored its prosperity. Yet this age of order declined when the country was overrun by invaders from the east called the Hyksos, who themselves founded a dynasty of kings. They introduced many new ideas and technological innovations into Egypt, in particular the horse and chariot.

The New Kingdom is generally regarded as Egypt's golden age, particularly the Eighteenth Dynasty, during which era some of the most celebrated monuments and works of art were produced. Ahmose, the founder of the dynasty, succeeded in expelling the Hyksos and his successors continued this tradition of military activity. By the reign of Ramesses II, Egypt had built up a sizeable empire and now had a standing army. Tribute money and diplomatic gifts from the Near East, the Aegean, and north-east Africa flowed into Egypt and the country's wealth was administered by a vast bureaucracy of literate officials and scribes. Some of the most famous rulers come from the Eighteenth Dynasty – King Akhenaten, who overturned established religious practice by introducing monotheism; the boy king Tutankhamun, whose splendid and virtually intact tomb treasures are unsurpassed; and Queen Hatshepsut, one of the few women to become pharaoh.

Ramesses II was the mightiest pharaoh of the New Kingdom, who built the most impressive monuments. He was over a hundred years old when he died and sired over a hundred children. Ramesses is frequently depicted in his chariot leading his army into battle and defeating Egypt's most

Granite head of Ramesses II from the Ramesseum near Thebes, once one of the most beautiful temples of Ancient Egypt.

The queen of Punt (second right) – clearly suffering from a form of steatopygia – was a visitor to Egypt during the reign of Queen Hatshepsut.

The Step Pyramid at Saqqara (opposite), designed by Imhotep in about 2580 BC as a tomb for Pharaoh Djoser, who died before its completion.

A view of part of the Ramesseum. Among the impressive monuments erected to Ramesses II there was a statue of the pharaoh about 17 metres high and weighing over 1000 tonnes.

traditional enemies – the Hittites and the Nubians. There were nine other kings called Ramesses, of which Ramesses III was the most notable. He built a fine temple complex at Medinet Habu and managed to defeat the Libyans and the so-called Sea Peoples of the Mediterranean. Around 1000 BC Egypt was divided between a dynasty of kings at Tanis in the Delta and the High Priests of Thebes. This political weakness led to foreign invasions by the Persians and Nubians, but the pharaohs of the Twenty-sixth Dynasty restored order and set up a new capital at Sais, where there was a renaissance in art. But this period of economic stability and strength came to an end and Egypt was invaded by a succession of foreign peoples including the Greeks, whose domination of Egypt, known as the Ptolemaic period, continued until Cleopatra was defeated at the Battle of Actium in 31 BC and Egypt became a province of the Roman Empire. Under the Romans, Christianity became the official Egyptian religion in AD 324, and in Egypt the Coptic church generated a distinctive style of art that subtly fused Egyptian, Greek and Roman elements.

After the Arab conquest in the seventh century and the country's conversion to Islam, Ancient Egypt became a "lost" and forgotten civilization for over a thousand years. The first major rediscovery occurred during Napoleon's Egyptian campaign in 1798. This was accompanied by an official expedition of scholars and artists, who recorded what they saw (it was eventually published in beautifully illustrated volumes called the *Description de L'Egypt*). At this time French soldiers found a granite slab at Rosetta, inscribed with a royal decree in three scripts – hieroglyphic, demotic (its cursive derivative) and Greek. Since ancient Greek was a known language, the importance of the Rosetta Stone was immediately recognized as the key to deciphering the "mysterious" hieroglyphs. It was, however, to take the French scholar Jean-François Champollion some twenty years of dedicated study to break the hieroglyphic code in 1822. Despite the lengthy and hazardous journey to Egypt in the nineteenth century, numerous Europeans were attracted to the country, not just out of curiosity, but for the opportunity to return with antiquities. This was a period when the great museums were being founded in major European cities and the fascination for ancient history led to a demand for Egyptian

The Rosetta Stone was inscribed with a royal decree from Ptolemaic Egypt in hieroglyphics (top), demotic (centre) and Greek (bottom). Its discovery led to the decipherment of the hitherto mysterious hieroglyphic script.

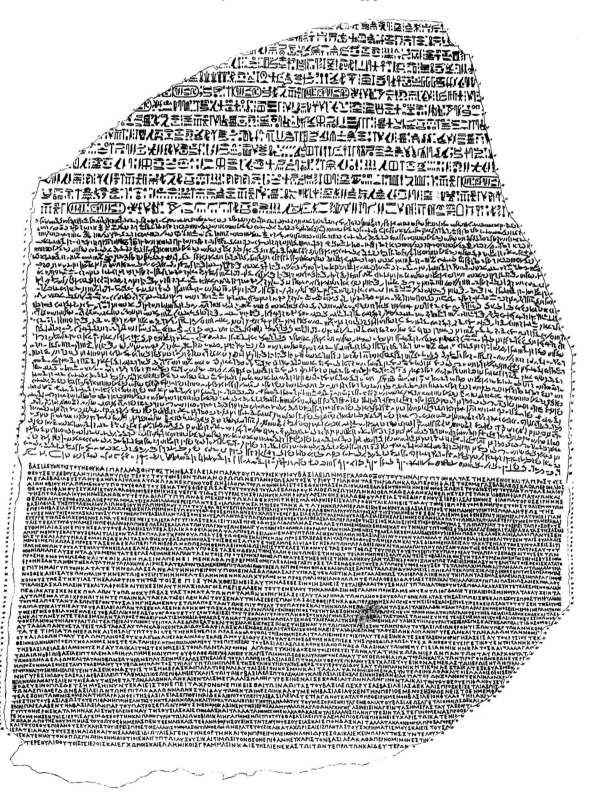

Treasure from the tomb of Tutankhamun, now held in the famous Cairo Museum. By the end of the 19th century the Museum was leading the way in the scientific archaeological exploration of Egypt's glorious past.

statues, mummies and tomb artefacts. To prevent indiscriminate looting of sites, an official Egyptian Government Antiquities Service was eventually set up by Auguste Mariette, who went on to found the first Cairo Museum in 1858. By the end of the nineteenth century a new standard of careful, scientific archaeology was practised and the most spectacular discovery was the tomb of King Tutankhamun in 1922, whose fantastic art treasures stunned the world.

Egyptian art is characterized by sculpture in the round, including statues, amulets and shabti tomb figurines. Stone was the most favoured material because of its monumental, enduring qualities, but wood and bronze, gold and faience were also used. Stone relief sculpture is also very typical, both raised and sunken relief or a combination of both. A preference for hard stones like granite gave Egyptian sculpture a static quality and preference for controlled, serene expression. However, with the Amarna style, during the reign of King Akhenaten, there was a tendency for increased naturalism and the pharaoh's strange appearance was considered an "art form". The paintings found in the tombs of royalty and the nobles were among Egypt's greatest artistic achievements. The walls of these tombs are covered with scenes from the everyday life of the owner and his wife, depicting his profession, family life and his most enjoyable pastimes such as hunting, fishing and banqueting. There are also scenes of agricultural life, craftsmen at work and servants, dancing girls, musicians, labourers, brewers and bakers, all intended for the well-being of the owner in the afterlife. The tomb was regarded as the "house" for the deceased to spend eternity and consequently the paintings represented the most enjoyable activities and an endless means of sustenance. The tomb owner and his family are shown as idealized humans, symbolic representations of the perfect rather than portraits. Accompanying most of the scenes are hieroglyphic texts, often providing a commentary, naming the owner with his title and biography and the essential magical formulas. By reciting these magical texts the paintings could be "brought to life" and thus the owner's existence was ensured for all eternity. Art was therefore a process of sympathetic magic and the artist paid great attention to representing the desired situation and material possessions in minute detail.

The extraordinary, characteristic Egyptian mode of depicting the human figure was also connected to magic. The head is nearly always shown in profile, but the eye is shown frontally. This convention was considered essential because if the head were shown frontally, the definition of the nose, symbolizing the breath of life, would be lost for all eternity, and so it is shown in profile. For magical reasons, as little as possible was omitted from the depiction and thus the afterlife. Therefore the shoulders

The stylized part-profile, part-frontal view of humans, characteristic of Egyptian art, was adopted for religious reasons. It was considered that symbolic features, including the nose in profile, had to be shown in order to ensure their power in the afterlife.

A wall painting from the tomb of the artisan Inherkha at Deir el-Medina, Luxor, shows women being entertained by a musician playing a harp.

and torso are shown from the front and in profile simultaneously while from the waist to the feet the figure is in profile, with the left foot forward. The concept of perspective is therefore missing from Egyptian painting.

Egyptian religion was at the very heart of the civilization. It revolved around the temple which was dedicated to the worship of a particular god or goddess. The priests enacted an elaborate daily ritual where the cult statue of a god was clothed in fresh linen and presented with offerings of food and drink. Since the temple was viewed as an image of the universe, ritual was believed to ensure the well-being and prosperity of the whole country, to maintain a sense of order above chaos. The Egyptians worshipped hundreds of different deities, most of whom were identified with an animal and were depicted as part-human and part-animal.

The most well-known Egyptian legend involved the life story of the god and legendary first king Osiris. He had triumphed over death and as such became associated with mummification and the Egyptian belief in an afterlife. The Osiris cycle ritual connected the Pharaoh with the powers of nature. Through the king all goodness and power flowed into the world and so all ceremonies were conducted in his name. The Egyptians thought that like Osiris they, too, could triumph over death and as such the body needed to be preserved to enable the soul to live forever. They consequently developed an elaborate embalming process that lasted seventy days. The mummy was then placed in the tomb with the dead person's favourite possessions and everything they needed for the next life. The Egyptians believed that you could take it all with you when you died. The body was also supplied with a copy of the *Book of the Dead*. This was actually a papyrus scroll that contained a number of spells to assist the deceased on the hazardous journey to the afterlife. This cult of the dead was ultimately responsible for preserving so much of Egyptian civilization for posterity.

Mythology is a timeless expression of human life and thought, as appealing and fascinating to us today as it was significant to the Egyptians whose religion it was so much a part of. Lewis Spence's *The Myths of Ancient*

The priesthood headed a religion that stood at the very heart of Egyptian civilization. Here a reproduction of an illustration from Thebes shows priests dressed in distinctive leopard skins.

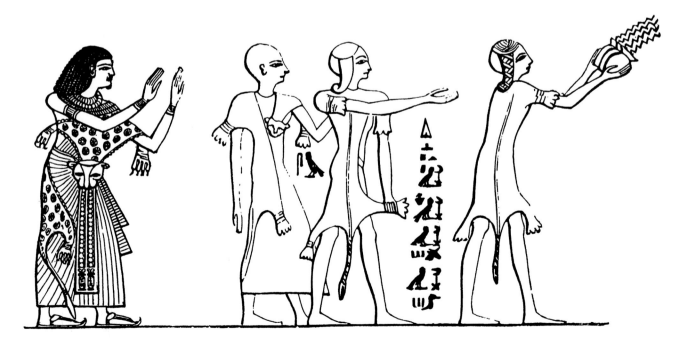

The Book of the Dead, a section of which is illustrated here, was a book of spells and guidance for use in the afterlife. A copy was always preserved with the mummy of the deceased.

Egypt, first published in 1915, is very much a classic work of its time, dedicated to what he called "the science of modern mythology". In order to comprehend the nature and development of early civilizations, it is useful to study many different examples, and he was fascinated by the universality of myth. A respected anthropologist, rather than Egyptologist, Spence was clearly inspired by the influential contemporary publication *The Golden Bough* (1914). This work by fellow anthropologist James Frazer tends to stress the psychological uniformity of all mankind and suggests that human groups evolve similar cultural patterns under similar circumstances. He was particularly interested in the Osiris myth, comparing it to Greek and Roman versions. Although such comparisons were popular with anthropologists at the time, it is still valuable to investigate the patterns that underlie the religious beliefs and myths of ancient cultures. The philosophical ideas that Egyptian mythology expresses anticipate those of the Greeks and even touch on certain aspects of Christian theology. Spence undoubtedly used Wallis Budge's celebrated 1903 publication *Studies in Egyptian Mythology* as the essential source for his research. Budge was a leading Egyptologist of his day and in charge of the British Museum's Egyptian Antiquities collection. Although somewhat outdated by modern Egyptological standards, it was a groundbreaking work based on his research into surviving Ancient Egyptian texts. With his impressive grasp of the scholarship of the time, enhanced with a remarkable knowledge of the myths of other cultures, Spence's text offers an unusual and useful insight into the subject.

CHAPTER I

THE WORLD OF EGYPTIAN MYTH

In an existence of some thousands of years, the group of beliefs which constituted what for convenience's sake is called the Egyptian religion passed through nearly every phase known to the student of comparative mythology. If the theologians of ancient Egypt found it impossible to form a pantheon of deities with any hope of consistency, assigning to each god or goddess his or her proper position in the divine galaxy as ruling over a definite sphere, cosmic or psychical, it may be asked in what manner the modern mythologist is better equipped to reduce to order elements so recondite as the mythic shapes of the divinities worshipped in the valley of the Nile.

But the answer is that the science of comparative religion has slowly diffused its light among the dark places of the ancient faiths. By the gleam of this magic lamp, then – more wonderful than any dreamt of by the makers of Eastern fable – let us walk in the gloom of the pyramids, in the cool shadows of ruined temples, aye, through the tortuous labyrinth of the Egyptian mind itself, trusting that by virtue of the light we carry we shall succeed in unravelling to some extent the age-long enigma of this mystical and mysterious land.

One of our first considerations must be that among such a concourse of gods as is presented by the Egyptian religion it would have been surprising if confusion had not arisen in the native mind concerning them. This is proved by the texts, which display in many cases much difficulty in defining the exact qualities of certain deities, their grouping and classification. The origin of this haziness is not far to seek. The deities of the

The Book of the Dead is an important guide to the deities of Ancient Egypt. In later versions up to 500 separate deities are identified.

A mummy case (opposite) decorated with a variety of magical symbols to protect the deceased in the afterlife. A deep pre-occupation with the afterlife was central to Egyptian mythology.

Each province or nome had its own deity, and even some individual villages such as Qurna, below the Sacred Mountain near the Valley of Kings (shown here), had local deities not worshipped elsewhere.

country multiplied at such an astonishing rate that whereas we find the texts of the early dynasties give us the names of some two hundred deities only, the later Theban Recension (or version) of the *Book of the Dead* supplies nearly five hundred, to which remain to be added the names of eight hundred further mythological beings.

Local Gods

Hathor, who appears here as the sacred Cow of Heaven bespangled with stars, was a popular goddess, and was worshipped in six separate nomes.

Another cause which made for confusion was that in every province and large town of Upper and Lower Egypt religion took what might almost be called a local form. The land of Egypt was divided into provinces called *hesput*, to which the Greeks gave the name of nome.

In each of these a certain god or group of gods held sway, the variation being caused by racial and other considerations. To the people of each nome their god was the deity par excellence, and in early times it is plain that the worship of each province amounted almost to a separate religion.

This division of the country must have taken place at an early epoch, and it contributed greatly to the long survival of such religious differences. The nome gods certainly date from pre-dynastic times, as is proved by inscriptions antedating the Pyramid Texts of the Fifth and Sixth Dynasties. The number of these provinces varied from one period to another, but the average seems to have been between thirty-five and forty. Several nomes worshipped the same god (for example, Horus was worshipped in not fewer than six, while in three provinces Khnemu was worshipped, and Hathor in six). But the great gods of the country were known by different names in each province, their ritual was distinctive, and even the legends of their origin and adventures assumed a different shape.

Many of the great cities, too, possessed special gods of their own, and to these were often added the attributes of one or more of the greater and more popular forms of godhead. Texts of all periods show that the chief local gods of many cities retained their pre-eminence almost to the end. The faith of the city that was the royal residence became the leading religion of the entire kingdom.

It might be expected that when Egypt attained a uniformity of culture, art, and nationhood, its religion would also become uniform and simplified. But such a consummation was never achieved. Even foreign intercourse failed almost entirely to break down the religious conservatism of priesthood and people. Indeed, the people may be said to have proved themselves more conservative than the priests. Alterations in religious policy, and differentiation in legend and hieratic texts, emanated from time to time from the various colleges of priests, or from the sovereign himself; but popular pressure seems always to have been in favour of the restitution of the traditional gods and forms of religion.

Local religious sites remained significant even after the unification of Egyptian culture, art and nationhood. The Sacred Pool at Karnak (below) continued to serve as such a site.

A canopic jar, used for the preservation of internal organs removed from a body undergoing mummification. Such care was typical of Egyptian attitudes to the afterlife.

Funerary Practices and the Gods of Egypt

We are ignorant of most of the gods worshipped during the first four dynasties, chiefly because of the lack of documentary evidence, although some are known from the inscription called the Palermo Stone, which alludes to several local deities. Some portions of the *Book of the Dead* may have been revised during the First Dynasty, and from this we may argue that the religion of the Egyptians during the first three dynasties closely resembled that revealed in the later texts.

It is only when we come to the Fifth and Sixth Dynasties that we discover material for the study of the Egyptian pantheon, in the Pyramid Texts of Unas, Teta, Pepi the First, and others. These texts are for the most part funerary, and it is through the examination of customs and beliefs relating to death and the afterlife that we can best approach Egyptian mythology as a whole.

No race conferred so much importance and dignity upon the cult of the dead as the Egyptian. It is dangerous to indulge in a universal assertion with reference to an entire nation, but if any people ever regarded life as a mere academy of preparation for eternity, it was this mysterious and fascinating race whose vast remains litter the banks of the world's most ancient river, and frown upon the less majestic undertakings of a civilization that has usurped the theatre of their myriad wondrous deeds.

Mummification

Egyptian religious tenets carefully fostered the idea of the preservation of the human body after death. Mummification was probably an invention of the Osirian cult. The priests of Osiris taught that the body of man was a sacred thing and not to be abandoned to the beasts of the desert, because from it would spring the effulgent and regenerated envelope of the purified spirit. In prehistoric times some attempt appears to have been made toward preservation, either by drying in the sun or smearing the corpse with a resinous preparation; and as the centuries went by this treatment developed into the elaborate art of embalming, with all its detailed ceremonial.

We do not find the process of mummification reaching any degree of elaboration until the period of the New Kingdom (c.1550–1086 BC). At first it was confined to the Pharaohs alone, who were identified with Osiris; but the necessity for a retinue who would attend him in the dark halls of the Duat (see page 25) prescribed that his courtiers also should be embalmed. The custom was taken up by the wealthy, and filtered down from rank to rank until at length even the corpse of the poorest Egyptian was at least subjected to a process of pickling in a bath of natron. The art of mummification reached its height in the Twenty-first Dynasty.

When the relations of the deceased consulted the professional embalmers they were shown models of mummies, one of which they selected. The corpse was then placed in the hands of the embalmers. First the brain and internal organs were removed. The body then underwent a drying process, and, according to the period, was stripped of its flesh, only the skin remaining, or was stuffed with sawdust, skilfully introduced through incisions, so that the natural form was completely restored. The cavity occupied by the organs might otherwise be stuffed with myrrh,

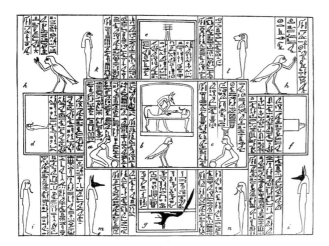

The Book of the Dead included extensive instructions on the process of mummification. Here Anubis, the jackal-headed god associated with mummification, is shown (centre) attending the mummy within the coffin chamber.

cassia, or other spices. When sewn up, the corpse was next pickled in a bath of natron for seventy days, and then meticulously bandaged with linen which had been dipped in some adhesive substance. A coffin was built which retained the shape of the human form, and which was elaborately painted with figures of divinities, amulets, symbols, and sometimes burial scenes. The carven countenance of the deceased surmounted this funerary finery, though the conventional death-mask in general bore but little resemblance to the person's likeness in life.

Funeral Offerings

The tomb furniture of the Egyptians of the higher ranks was elaborate and costly – chairs, jars, weapons, mirrors, sometimes even chariots, and wigs. Beginning with the Middle Kingdom (Eighteenth Dynasty), small statuettes, called ushabtiu, were placed in each tomb. These represented various trades, and were supposed to assist or serve the deceased in the other world. The walls of the tomb and the sides of the sarcophagus were usually covered with texts from the *Book of the Dead*, or formulae devoting offerings of loaves, geese, beer, and other provisions to the ka (see below) of the deceased.

The burial ceremony was stately and imposing. Sometimes it chanced that the corpse had to be conveyed by water, and gaily painted boats held the funeral procession; or else the chain of mourners moved slowly along by the western bank of the Nile.

The ceremonial at the tomb symbolized the night journey of Ra-Osiris The kinsmen of the deceased were assisted in the procession by a professional class of mourners. The corpse was taken from the coffin, and was placed upright against the wall of the tomb by a priest wearing the mask of the jackal-headed god Anubis. At this point an elaborate ceremony was performed, known as the "opening of the mouth". With many magical spells and signs the mouth of the deceased was opened with a hook, to enable him to speak, eat, and drink in the afterlife. This ceremonial was interminable in the case of a person of importance, at least twenty-eight formulae having to be recited, many of which were accompanied by lustration, purification, and, on the part of the priests who officiated, a change of costume. The coffin containing the mummy was then lowered into the tomb by a long rope, and was received by the grave-diggers.

The mythological journey of Ra-Osiris, the sun god, on his nightly passage through the Duat (underworld) underlay the ceremonies performed at tombs. Here the god travels on the night-boat along the river of the Duat, accompanied by other gods and goddesses.

The Ka and the Ba

The dead man or woman was practically at the mercy of the living for subsistence in the other world. Unless his kinsmen continued their offerings to him, his ka would starve. This ka was his double, and came into the world at the same time as himself. It must be sharply distinguished from the ba, or soul, which usually took the form of a bird and took wing after the death of its owner.

Some Egyptologists consider the ka to be the special active force which imbues the human being with life, and it may be equivalent to the Hebrew expression "spirit" as apart from "soul". When a person died their ka quitted the body, but did not cease to take an interest in it, and on occasion even reanimated it. It was on behalf of the ka that Egyptian tombs were so well furnished with food and drink, and the necessities, not to say the luxuries, of existence.

The *Book of the Dead*

The *Book of the Dead*, the Egyptian title of which, *Pert em hru*, has been variously translated "coming forth by day" and the "manifestation day", is a great body of religious compositions compiled for the use of the dead in the other world. It is also an allegory of the passage of the sun through the underworld after it has set each day. These two concepts are inextricably bound together in Egyptian mythology.

Texts dealing with the welfare of the dead and their life in the world beyond the grave are known to have been in use among the Egyptians as early as 4000 BC. Dr Budge states: "We are in any case justified in estimating the earliest form of the work to be contemporaneous with the foundation of the civilization which we call 'Egyptian' in the valley of the Nile." The oldest versions of the *Book of the Dead* are contained in the early Pyramid Texts, but with the invention of mummification a more complete funerary ritual arose, based on the hope that such ceremonies would ensure the corpse against corruption, preserve it for ever, and introduce it to a beatified existence among the gods.

There were three recensions (or versions) of the *Book of the Dead* – the Heliopolitan, the Theban, and the Saite. The Heliopolitan Recension was found in the Pyramid Texts of Unas, Teta, and Pepi, and represents the theological system introduced by the priests of Ra; the essentials of the primitive Egyptian religion are, however, retained. In later times the priesthood of Ra was forced to acknowledge the supremacy of Osiris, and this theological defeat is visible in the more modern texts.

The Theban Recension was current from the Eighteenth to the Twenty-second Dynasties, and was usually written upon papyri and painted upon coffins in hieroglyphs. Each chapter was preserved as a separate entity, apparently with no overall scheme of arrangement being agreed.

The Saite Recension was definitely arranged prior to the Twenty-sixth Dynasty, and is written upon coffins and papyri, and also in hieratic and demotic script. It continued to be employed to the end of the Ptolemaic period of Egyptian history.

Reeds grow in great profusion in the Nile valley, and the Field of Reeds, an important part of the Duat, gave the mythological underworld a quality of familiarity to the Egyptians.

The *Book of the Dead* was for the use of the deceased from the moment when he found himself an inhabitant of the other world. Magic was the very mainspring of existence in that sphere, and unless a spirit was acquainted with the formulae that compelled the respect of the various gods and demons, and even of inanimate objects, it was helpless.

The region to which the dead departed was called the Duat by the primitive Egyptians. It was regarded as dark and gloomy, containing pits of fire and dreadful monsters, and was bounded by a river and a lofty chain of mountains. The part of it that was nearest to Egypt was regarded as a description of mingled desert and forest, through which the soul of the deceased might not hope to struggle unless guided by some benevolent spirit who knew the path. Darkness covered everything, and the inhabitants of the place practised all sorts of hostility toward the new-comer.

But there was one desirable part in this horrid region – the Sekhet Hetepet, the Elysian fields, which contained the Sekhet Aaru, or the Field of Reeds, where dwelt the god Osiris and his company. At first he had domain over this part of the Duat alone, but gradually he succeeded in extending it over the entire country of the dead, of which he was monarch. The wish of all Egyptians was to win through to the kingdom of Osiris, and to that end they made an exhaustive study of the *Book of the Dead*.

The Field of Reeds

We learn from the Theban Recension that there were seven halls or mansions in the Field of Reeds, all of which the soul had to pass through before it was received by the god in person. Three gods guarded the door of each hall – the doorkeeper, watchman, and questioner. It was necessary for the new-comer to address each god by his name, which was actually a spell consisting of a number of words.

The Field of Reeds was divided into fifteen regions, each of which was presided over by a god. The first of these regions was called Amentet, where dwelt those souls who lived upon earth-offerings. The second was Sekhet Aaru, the Field of Reeds proper, the surrounding walls of which were formed of the same stuff as that which makes up the sky. Here dwelt the souls, who were nine cubits high, under the rule of Ra-Heru-Khuti, and this place was the centre of the kingdom of Osiris. The third was the place of the spirit-souls, a region of fire. In the fourth dwelt the terrible serpent

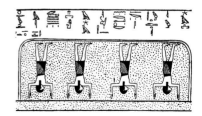

The third region of the Field of Reeds was a fearsome place in which the damned were immersed headfirst in pits of fire.

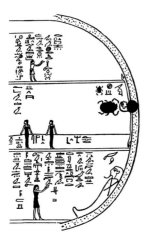

At the eastern end of the Duat the mummified body of the sun god waits while the beetle Khepra, deity of the rising sun, pushes the solar disk out of the Duat into the new day.

The falcon-headed Seker, another god associated with funerary rites, had his own realm within the Duat. His appearance in the night journey of Ra-Osiris emphasizes the cumulative tendency of much Egyptian mythology.

Sati-temui, which preyed on the dead who dwelt in the Duat. The fifth region was inhabited by spirits who fed upon the shadows of the weak and helpless souls. The remaining regions were of a similar nature.

The Journey of Osiris

We find other descriptions of the Duat in the *Book of Gates* and the *Book of Him who is in the Duat*, in which is outlined the journey that the sun-god (combining elements of both Ra and Osiris) makes through the other world after he has set upon the earth. His entrance to the antechamber of the Duat in the west is heralded by songs of praise, raised by the ape-gods, while serpents blow fire from their mouths by the light of which his pilot-gods steer his craft. All the doors are thrown open, and the dead, revived by the earthly air that the god carries with him, come to life again for a brief hour. All the creatures of this portion of the Duat are provided with meat and drink by command of the god. Such of the dead as dwell here are those who have failed to pass the various tests for entrance to his court, and all that they exist for is the material comfort provided by the brief diurnal passage of the deity.

When the sun-god, who in this form is known as Af-Ra, reaches the entrance to the second part of the Duat, which is called Urnes, the gods of the first station depart from him, and do not again behold his face until the following night. At this point the boat of Af-Ra is met by the boats of Osiris and his attendant gods, and in this place also he orders that the dead should receive food, light, and air. Here he grapples with the serpents Hau and Neha-her, and, having overcome them, is led into the Field of the Grain-gods, where he reposes for a while. While there he hearkens to the prayers of the living on behalf of the dead, and takes account of the offerings made for them. Continuing his journey, he traverses the twelve sections of the Duat. In some of these we see what were probably quite separate realms of the dead, such as the Realm of Seker, a god who is perhaps of greater antiquity than Osiris. The sun-god passes through this place by subterranean passages, from which he emerges into Amhet, where is situated a stream of boiling water. But he is not out of the kingdom of Seker until he reaches the sixth section, where dwell the dead kings of Egypt and the Khu or Spirit-souls.

It is at this point of his journey that Af-Ra turns his face toward the east and directs his course to the Mountain of the Sunrise; previous to this he has been journeying from the south to the north. In the seventh section he is joined by Isis and other deities, and here his path is obstructed by the wicked serpent Apep, through whose body the attendant deities drive their daggers. A company of gods tow him through the eighth section, but his vessel sails itself through the ninth, and in the tenth and eleventh he seems to pass over a series of lakes, which may represent the lagoons of the eastern delta. In the latter section his progress is lighted by a disk of light, encircled by a serpent, which rests upon the prow of the boat. The twelfth section contains the great mass of celestial waters called Nu, and here dwells Nut, the personification of the morning. Before the boat looms the great serpent Ankh-neteru, and twelve of the gods, taking hold of the tow-line, enter this serpent at the tail and draw the god in his boat through the monstrous body, bringing Af-Ra out at its mouth; but not as Af-Ra, for during this passage he has been transformed into Khepra, in whose shape he is towed into the sky by twelve goddesses, who lead him before Shu, the god of the atmosphere of the terrestrial world.

Shu places him in an opening in the semicircular wall that forms the end of the twelfth section, and he now appears to mortal eyes as a disk of light, having discarded his mummified form, in which he traversed the Duat. His progress is followed by the acclamations of his company of gods, who fall upon and destroy his enemies and sing hymns of praise to him.

The twelfth region of the Duat was the home of the goddess Nut, symbolic of the morning sky being lifted, as represented here, from the body of the earth.

Osiris the Judge

It was only during the Middle Kingdom that the conception of Osiris as judge of the dead took definite form and received general recognition. In one of the chapters of the *Book of the Dead* we find him seated in a large hall, the roof of which is covered with fire and symbols of truth. Before him are the symbol of Anubis, the four sons of Horus, and the Devourer of the West, a monster who serves as his protector. In the rear sit the forty-two judges of the dead. The deceased makes his appearance before the god and his heart is placed in a great balance to be weighed by Anubis, Thoth, the scribe of the gods, standing by to note the result upon his tablets. the result is communicated to Osiris, and the dead man, if found worthy, is presented to

The jackal-headed Anubis, shown attending a mummy in a painting from the tomb of the artisan Inherkha at Deir el-Medina, Luxor, also acted as judge of the dead.

the deity, to whom he repeats a long prayer, in which he states that he has not committed any evil. Those who could not pass the test were hurried away, and were apparently in danger of being devoured by a frightful monster called Beby, which awaited them outside.

The justified deceased took part in the life of Osiris and the other gods. This life is outlined in an inscription on the tomb of Paheri, prince of El Kab, as follows:

"Thou goest in and out with a glad heart, and with the rewards of the gods.... Thou becomest a living soul; thou hast power over bread, water, and air. Thou changest thyself into a phoenix or a swallow, a sparrow-hawk or a heron, as thou desirest. Thou dost cross in the boat and art not hindered. Thou sailest upon the water when a flood ariseth. Thou livest anew and thy soul is not parted from thy body. Thy soul is a god together with the illuminated, and the excellent souls speak with thee. Thou art among them and (verily) receivest what is given upon earth; thou possessest water, possessest air, hast superabundance of that which thou desirest. Thine eyes are given to thee to see, and thine ears to hear speech, thy mouth speaketh, thy legs move, thy hands and arms bestir themselves

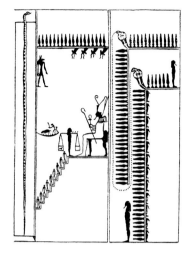

Osiris, seated in the Hall of Judgement with the scales in which the heart of the deceased is weighed before him, addressed by Anubis (top left): a reproduction from the sarcophagus in the Soane Museum, London.

for thee, thy flesh grows, thy veins are in health, and thou feelest thyself well in all thy limbs. Thou hast thine upright heart in thy possession, and thy earlier heart belongs to thee. Thou dost mount up to heaven and art summoned each day to the libation table of Wennofre, thou receivest the good which has been offered to him and the gifts of the Lords of the necropolis."

It has been suggested that the *Book of the Dead* may have been the ritual of a secret brotherhood, and that the various halls mentioned in it symbolized the several stages of initiation through which the members had to pass. The mysteries of Eleusis, and similar Greek initiatory ceremonies, included a theatric representation of the wanderings of the mother in search of her daughter in the underworld. If the *Book of the Dead* did not contain an early type of initiatory ceremonial, it may have powerfully influenced the ceremonial of such mysteries when they arose. On the other hand, the *Book of the Dead* may represent the ceremonial of a much older prehistoric mystery that had been forgotten by the dynastic Egyptians. It may preserve a Neolithic ritual, originating thousands of years before its connection with the worship of Osiris.

Anubis oversees the weighing of the heart of the deceased, with the ibis-headed Thoth recording the result and a part-lion, part-crocodile, part-hippopotamus monster waiting to devour those who fail the test. The deceased is presented to Osiris (right) by Horus.

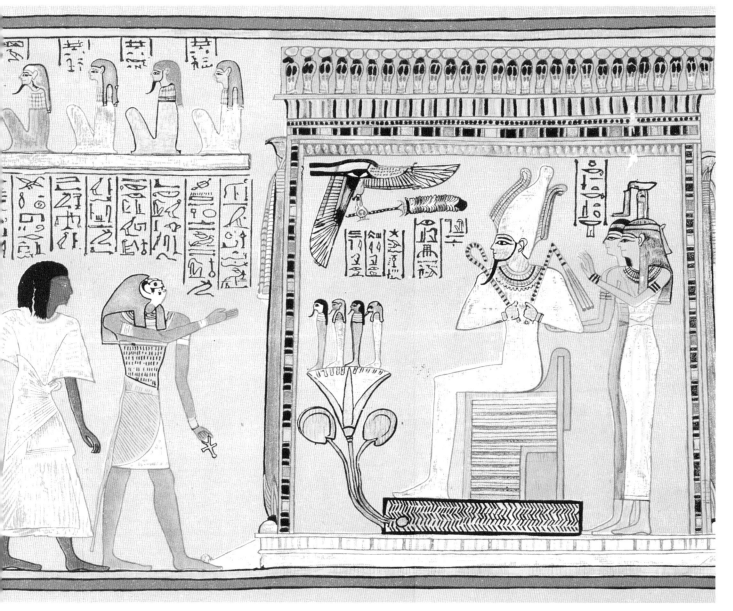

CHAPTER II

THE GODS AND GODDESSES OF EGYPT

OSIRIS

One of the principal figures in the Egyptian pantheon, and one whose elements it is most difficult to disentangle, is Osiris, or As-ar. In dynastic times Osiris was regarded as god of the dead and the underworld. Indeed, he occupied the same position in that sphere as Ra did in the land of the living.

The origins of the cult of Osiris are extremely obscure. We cannot glean from the texts when or where he first began to be worshipped, but that his cult is greatly more ancient than any text is certain. The earliest dynastic centres of his worship were Abydos and Mendes. He is perhaps represented on a mace-head of Narmer found at Hieraconpolis, and on a wooden plaque of the reign of Udy-mu (Den) or Wesepti, the fifth king of the First Dynasty, who is figured as dancing before him. This shows that a centre of Osiris worship existed at Abydos during the First Dynasty. But allusions in the Pyramid Texts give us to understand that prior to this shrines had been raised to Osiris in various parts of the Nile country.

According to the *Book of the Dead*, Osiris dwells peaceably in the underworld with the justified, judging the souls of the departed as they appear before him. This paradise was known as Aaru, and although it was situated in the underworld, it was originally thought to be in the sky.

Osiris is usually shown wrapped in mummy bandages and wearing the white cone-shaped crown of the South, and he appears to be Libyan in origin. Brugsch and Maspero both regarded him as a water-god, the creative and nutritive powers of the Nile stream in general, and of the inundation in particular. But if Osiris is a god of the Nile, why import him from the Libyan desert, which is of course entirely without rivers?

Sir James Frazer on Osiris

From the particulars of the Osiris myth Sir James Frazer argued that Osiris was "one of those personifications of vegetation whose annual death and resurrection have been celebrated in so many lands" – that he was a god of vegetation analogous to Adonis and Attis.

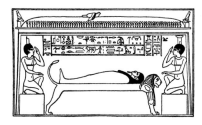

Osiris of Abydos, shown in his characteristic mummy bandages and laid out on a bed as a corpse. Osiris may have been worshipped at Abydos as early as the First Dynasty.

The Temple of Isis and Osiris at Philae (opposite) was painstakingly moved to a new site when the High Dam at Aswan was constructed in the 1960s. Philae was one of the most important centres of the cult of Osiris.

Osiris seated in his shrine at Abydos, attended by goddesses. He wears the cone-shaped crown of Upper Egypt.

Peasants reaping corn in a painting from the tomb of the artisan Sennedjen at Deir el-Medina, Luxor. Osiris was believed to have taught Egyptians the cultivation of corn.

"The general similarity of the myth and ritual of Osiris to those of Adonis and Attis," says Frazer, "is obvious. In all three cases we see a god whose untimely and violent death is mourned by a loving goddess and annually celebrated by his worshippers. The character of Osiris as a deity of vegetation is brought out by the legend that he was the first to teach men the use of corn, and by the custom of beginning his annual festival with the tillage of the ground. He is also said to have introduced the cultivation of the vine. In one of the chambers dedicated to Osiris in the great temple of Isis at Philae the dead body of Osiris is represented with stalks of corn springing from it, and a priest is depicted watering the stalks from a pitcher which he holds in his hand. The accompanying legend sets forth that 'this is the form of him whom one may not name, Osiris of the mysteries, who springs from the returning waters.' It would seem impossible to devise a more graphic way of depicting Osiris as a personification of the corn; the inscription attached to the picture proves that this personification was the kernel of the mysteries of the god, the innermost secret that was only revealed to the initiated. In estimating the mythical character of Osiris, very great weight must be given to this monument. The story that his mangled remains were scattered up and down the land may be a mythical way of

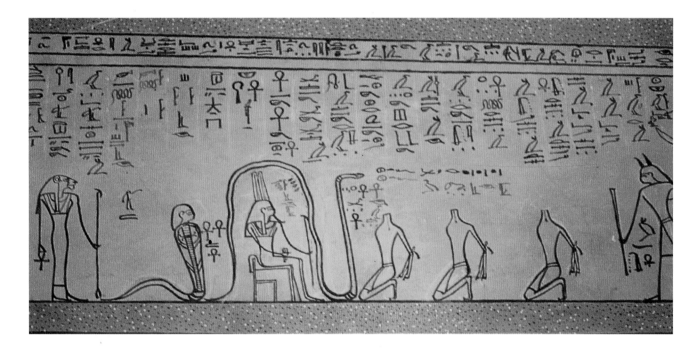

expressing either the sowing or the winnowing of the grain. The latter interpretation is supported by the tale that Isis placed the severed limbs of Osiris on a corn-sieve."

Or the legend may be a reminiscence of the custom of slaying a human victim as a representative of the corn-spirit, and distributing his flesh or scattering his ashes over the fields to fertilize them.

"But Osiris was more than a spirit of the corn; he was also a tree-spirit, and this may well have been his original character, since the worship of trees is naturally older in the history of religion than the worship of the cereals. His character as a tree-spirit was represented very graphically in a ceremony described by Firmicus Maternus. A pine-tree having been cut down, the centre was hollowed out, and with the wood thus excavated an image of Osiris was made, which was then 'buried' in the hollow of the tree. Here, again, it is hard to imagine how the conception of a tree as tenanted by a personal being could be more plainly expressed. The image of Osiris thus made was kept for a year and then burned, exactly as was done with the image of Attis which was attached to the pine-tree. The ceremony of cutting the tree, as described by Firmicus Maternus, appears to be alluded to by Plutarch. It was probably the ritual counterpart of the mythical discovery of the body of Osiris enclosed in the erica tree. We may conjecture that the erection of the Tatu pillar at the close of the annual festival of Osiris was identical to the ceremony described by Firmicus; it is to be noted that in the myth the erica tree formed a pillar in the king's house. Like the similar custom of cutting a pine-tree and fastening an image to it, in the rites of Attis, the ceremony perhaps belonged to the class of customs of which the bringing in of the Maypole is among the most familiar. As to the pine-tree in particular, at Denderah the tree of Osiris is a conifer and the coffer containing the body of Osiris is here depicted as enclosed within the tree. A pine-cone often appears on the monuments as an offering presented to Osiris, and a manuscript in the Louvre speaks of the cedar as sprung from him. The sycamore and the tamarisk are also his trees. In inscriptions he is spoken of as residing in them, and his mother Nut is frequently portrayed

The association of Osiris with bodily dismemberment was clearly a powerful one in Egypt. Here the god is sheltered by a serpent which consumes the decapitated bodies of the damned in the Duat.

The erica tree in which the body of Osiris was concealed became a widespread symbol of the god: here the soul of Osiris is shown above the tree (left).

Denderah was an important site of worship of the goddess Hathor, but it also contained the so-called Tomb of Osiris, in which his death and resurrection were celebrated.

in a sycamore. In a sepulchre at How (Diospolis Parva) a tamarisk is depicted overshadowing the coffer of Osiris; and in the series of sculptures that illustrate the mystic history of Osiris in the great temple of Isis at Philae a tamarisk is figured with two men pouring water on it. The inscription on this last monument leaves no doubt, says Brugsch, that the verdure of the earth was believed to be connected with the verdure of the tree, and that the sculpture refers to the grave of Osiris at Philae, of which Plutarch tells us that it was overshadowed by a methide plant, taller than any olive-tree. This sculpture, it may be observed, occurs in the same chamber in which the god is depicted as a corpse with ears of corn sprouting from him. In inscriptions he is referred to as 'the one in the tree', 'the solitary one in the acacia', and so forth. On the monuments he sometimes appears as a mummy covered with a tree or with plants. It accords with the character of Osiris as a tree-spirit that his worshippers were forbidden to injure fruit-trees, and with his character as a god of vegetation in general that they were not allowed to stop up wells of water, which are so important for the irrigation of hot southern lands."

Frazer goes on to combat the theory that Osiris was to be identified with the sun god Ra. Osiris, says the German scholar Lepsius, was named Ra-Osiris even in the *Book of the Dead*, and Isis, his spouse, is often called the royal consort of Ra. This identification, Frazer thinks, may have had a political significance. He admits that the myth of Osiris might express the

daily appearance and disappearance of the sun, and points out that most of the writers who favour the solar theory are careful to indicate that it is the daily, and not the annual, course of the sun to which they understand the myth to apply. But then why, asks Frazer, was it celebrated by an annual ceremony? "This fact alone seems fatal to the interpretation of the myth as descriptive of sunset and sunrise. Again, though the sun may be said to die daily, in what sense can it be said to be torn in pieces?"

Osiris was sometimes associated with the moon. Here an illustration from Denderah shows the god with a lunar symbol.

Osiris and the Moon

Plutarch says that some of the Egyptian philosophers interpreted Osiris as the moon; "because the moon, with her humid and generative light, is favourable to the propagation of animals and the growth of plants." In many early mythologies the moon is regarded as a great source of moisture. Vegetation is thought to flourish beneath her pale rays, and she is understood as fostering the multiplication of the human species as well as of animal and plant life. Frazer enumerates several reasons to prove that Osiris possessed a lunar significance. Briefly these are that he is said to have lived or reigned for twenty-eight years, the mythical expression of a lunar month, and that his body is said to have been cut into fourteen pieces – "This might be interpreted as the waning moon, which appears to lose a portion of itself on each of the fourteen days that make up the second half of the lunar month." Set (who took the form of an evil deity, see page 46) found the body of Osiris at the full moon; thus its dismemberment would begin with the waning of the moon.

Frazer quotes Plutarch to the effect that at the new moon of the month of Phanemoth, which was the beginning of spring, the Egyptians celebrated what they called "the entry of Osiris into the moon"; that at the ceremony called the "Burial of Osiris" they made a crescent-shaped chest, "because the moon when it approaches the sun assumes the form of a crescent and vanishes"; and that once a year, at the full moon, pigs (possibly symbolic of Set) were sacrificed simultaneously to the moon and to Osiris.

In effect, then, Frazer's theory is that Osiris was a vegetation or corn god, who later became identified, or confused, with the moon. But surely it is as reasonable to suppose that it was because of his status as moon-god that he ranked as a deity of vegetation? A brief consideration of the circumstances connected with lunar worship might lead us to some such supposition. The sun in its status of deity requires little explanation. The phenomena of growth are attributed to its agency at an early period of human thought, and it is probable that wind, rain, and other atmospheric manifestations are likewise credited to the sun's action, or regarded as emanations from it. By analogy, the moon also comes to be regarded as an agency of growth, and powers are attributed to it almost equal to those of the sun.

The importance of the sun, shown here rising behind the Temple of Isis at Philae, in Egyptian mythology cannot be underestimated. But the power of the moon was thought to equal that of the sun on the cycles of growth.

It must also be borne in mind that the moon is regarded as the great reservoir of magical power. In the Libyan desert at night the moon is an object which dominates the entire landscape, and it is difficult to believe that its intense brilliance and all-pervading light would not have deeply impressed the wandering tribes of that region with a sense of reverence and worship. Indeed, reverence for such an object might well precede the worship of a mere corn and tree spirit, who in such surroundings could not have much scope for the manifestation of his powers. We can see, then, that such a moon-god of the Neolithic Nubians, imported into a more fertile land, would speedily become identified with the powers of growth through moisture, and thus with the Nile itself.

Osiris, in his character as god of the dead, combines all the ideas of the moon, moisture, the underworld, and death – in fact, all the phenomena of birth and decay.

Osiris and the Persephone Myth

There is a very close resemblance between the myth of Osiris and that of the Classical goddesses Demeter and Kore, or Persephone. Indeed, some of the adventures of Isis, notably that concerning the child of the king of Byblos, are practically identical with incidents in the career of Demeter. It is highly probable that the two myths possessed a common origin. But whereas in the Greek example we find the mother searching for her child, in the Egyptian myth the wife searches for the remains of her husband. In the Greek tale we have Pluto as the husband of Persephone and the ruler of the underworld also regarded, like Osiris, as a god of grain and growth, whilst Persephone, like Isis, probably personifies the grain itself. It would seem that the Hellenic myth had been sophisticated by early Egyptian influences, perhaps through a Cretan intercommunication.

It remains to consider Osiris as ruler of the underworld. The god of the underworld is in nearly every instance a god of vegetable growth, and it was not because Osiris was god of the dead that he presided over fertility, but the converse. Osiris was first god of fertility, and his association with the underworld was a later innovation: but it was a logical outcome of his status as god of growth.

The extraordinary fertility of Egypt was totally dependent on the Nile, and it is possible that the early Nubian Osiris as a moon and fertility god became closely associated with the river when translated into Egyptian religion.

A New Osirian Theory

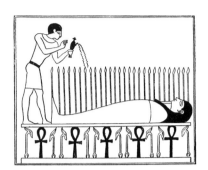

Shoots of corn sprouting from the body of Osiris, reproduced from a relief at Philae. The corn shoots may symbolize resurrection rather than suggesting that Osiris was a god of grain.

We must also take into brief consideration his personification of Ra, whom he meets, blends with, and under whose name he nightly sails through his own dominions. This would seem like the fusion of a sun and moon myth; the myth of the sun travelling nightly beneath the earth fused with that of the moon's nocturnal journey across the vault of heaven. A moment's consideration will show how this fusion took place. Ra, the sun-god, must perambulate the underworld at night if he is to appear on the fringes of the east in the morning. But Osiris, in his character as god of the underworld, is already occupying the orbit Ra must trace. The orbits of both deities are fused in one, and there would appear to be some proof of this in the fact that, in the realm of Seker, Af-Ra (or Ra-Osiris) changes the direction of his journey from north to south to a line due east toward the mountains of sunrise. The fusion of the two myths is quite a logical one, as the moon during the night travels in the same direction as the sun has taken during the day – that is, from east to west.

It will readily be seen how Osiris came to be regarded not only as god and judge of the dead, but also as symbolic of the resurrection of the body of man. Frazer lays great stress upon a picture of Osiris in which his body is shown covered with sprouting shoots of corn, which he takes as evidence that Osiris was a corn god. In our view the picture is simply symbolic of resurrection. The circumstance that Osiris is represented in the picture as in the recumbent position of the dead lends added weight to this supposition, and the corn-shoot is a world-wide symbol of resurrection. Later the vegetation myth clustering round Osiris was metamorphosed into a theological tenet regarding human resurrection, and Osiris was believed to have been once a human being who had died and had been dismembered. His body, however, was made whole again by Isis, Anubis, and Horus, acting upon the instructions of Thoth. A good deal of magical ceremony appears to have been mingled with the process, and this in turn was utilized in the case of every dead Egyptian by the priests in connection with the embalmment and burial of the dead in the hope of resurrection. Osiris, however, was regarded as the principal cause of human resurrection, and he was capable of giving life after death because he had attained to it. He was entitled "Eternity and Everlastingness", and he it was who made men and women to be born again. This conception of resurrection appears to have been in vogue in Egypt from very early times. The great authority upon Osiris is the *Book of the Dead*, which might well be called the "Book of Osiris", and in which are recounted his daily doings and his nightly journeyings in his kingdom of the underworld.

ISIS

Isis, or Ast, must be regarded as one of the earliest and most important goddesses of ancient Egypt. In the dynastic period she was regarded as the feminine counterpart of Osiris, and we may take it that before the dawn of Egyptian history she occupied a similar position. No other deity has been

Isis, the feminine counterpart of Osiris, suckles their son Horus: a relief from the Temple of Isis at Denderah.

worshipped for such an extent of time, for her cult did not perish with that of most other Egyptian gods, but flourished later in Greece and Rome, and was seriously carried on in Paris at the end of the nineteenth century.

Isis was perhaps of Libyan origin, and is usually depicted in the form of a woman crowned with her name-symbol and holding in her hand a sceptre of papyrus. Her crown is surmounted by a pair of horns holding a disk, which in turn is sometimes crested by her hieroglyph, which represents a seat or throne. Sometimes also she is represented as possessing radiant and many-coloured wings, with which she stirs to life the inanimate body of Osiris.

No other goddess was on the whole so popular with the Egyptians, perhaps because of the circumstances of travail and pity that run through her myth. But she was also the great and beneficent mother-goddess and represented the maternal spirit in its most intimate and affectionate guise. In her myth, perhaps one of the most touching and beautiful that ever sprang from the consciousness of a people, we find evolved from what may have been a mere corn-spirit a type of wifely and maternal affection mourning the death of her cherished husband, and seeking by every means in her power to restore him to life.

The cult of Isis underwent a major revival in Greece and Rome after the decline of Ancient Egypt. This statue of Isis was found at a temple in Pompeii.

Isis as a swallow, in which form she restored Osiris back to life by fanning him with her wings and filling his nostrils with air.

Isis as the Wind

Although Isis had undoubtedly many forms, the probabilities are that in one of her phases she represents the wind of heaven. Osiris, in his guise of the corn, dies and comes to life again and is sown broadcast over the land. Isis is disconsolate and moans terribly over his death; in fact, so loud and heartrending is her grief that the child of the King of Byblos, whom she is nursing, dies of terror. She is perfumed, as the women of the Queen of Byblos experience. She transforms herself into a swallow. She restores the dead Osiris to life by fanning him with her wings and filling his mouth and nostrils with sweet air. She is one of the few Egyptian deities who possess wings, and is a great traveller. All these qualities suggest the wind. Isis wails like the wind, she shrieks in tempest, she carries the fragrance of

Isis is often associated with Maat, the goddess of justice, illustrated here wearing her characteristic ostrich feather headdress.

spices and flowers throughout the country, she takes the shape of a swallow, one of the swiftest of birds and typical of the rapidity of the wind, she employs the element of which she is mistress to revivify the dead Osiris, she possesses wings, as do all deities connected with the wind, and she is constantly travelling up and down the land. In one of her phases she certainly typifies the revivifying power of the spring wind, which wails over the grave of the sleeping grain, bringing reanimating breath to the inert seeds.

Isis was one of those deities fated to achieve greatness. She rose to such supreme importance during her reign of nearly four thousand years in Egypt that every description or attribute was heaped upon her in abundance, including some actually at variance with her original character. Isis is a giver of life and food to the dead in the Duat – that is, she brings with her the fresh air of heaven into the underworld – and is identified with Maat, the goddess of justice.

Isis may also typify the wind of morning, from which the sun is born. In most countries at the moment of sunrise a wind springs up which may be said to usher the sun into existence. In her myth, too, we find that on leaving the house where she had been imprisoned by Set (the summer dwelling of the wind, which during that season leaves Egypt altogether) she is preceded by seven scorpions, the fierce-stinging blasts of winter. They show her the way through swamps and marshes. Women shut the doors in her face; a child is stung by one of the scorpions, but Isis restores it to life – that is, the child recovers with the approach of better weather. Her own son Horus is stung by a scorpion – that is, the heat of the sun is rendered weak by the cold of winter until it is restored by Isis, the genial spring wind.

Attributes of Isis

Isis was also a powerful enchantress, as is shown by the number of deities and human beings whom she rescued from death. Her astronomical symbol was the star Sept, which marked the spring and the approach of the inundation of the Nile, an added evidence that in one of her phases she was goddess of the winds of spring. As the light-giver at this season of the year she was called Khut, and as goddess of the fruitful earth Usert. As the force which impelled the powers of spring and sent forth the Nile flood she was Sati, and as the goddess of fertile waters she was Anqet. She was further the deity of cultivated lands and fields, goddess of harvest and goddess of food. She personifies the power of the spring season, the power of the earth to grow and yield grain, motherhood and all the attributes and affinities which spring therefrom. The strength of her cult is evinced by the fact that it was not finally deserted in Egypt until the middle of the fifth century AD.

As the goddess of harvests and food, Isis is depicted giving bread and water to the bird symbolizing the soul of the deceased.

HORUS

The falcon normally symbolizes the sun god Ra, but there was another god of similar form who had been worshipped before him in the land of Egypt. This was the god Heru, or Horus, "He who is above". This god had many

shapes. As Horus the Elder he is depicted as a man with the head of a falcon, and was believed to be the son of Geb and Nut. Horus proper was perhaps regarded as the face of heaven, the countenance of the sky, and as Horus the Elder he represented the face by day in contradistinction to Set, who was the face by night.

Horus the Younger, or Harpocrates as he was called by the Greeks, is represented as a youth, and was the son of the goddess Rat-Tauit, who appears to have been worshipped at Hermonthis in the form of a hippopotamus. Horus the Younger represented the earliest rays of the rising sun, and had no fewer than seven aspects or forms.

Horus of the Two Horizons, the Harmachis of the Greeks, was one of the chief forms of the sun-god Ra, and represented the sun in his diurnal course from sunrise to sunset. He thus included the personalities of Ra, Tem, and Khepra, and this affords a good example of the widespread system of overlapping that occurred in Egyptian mythology. Probably a number of these Horus-gods were local. Thus we find Harmachis worshipped principally at Heliopolis and Apollinopolis. His best-known monument is the famous Sphinx, near the pyramids of Gizeh.

The falcon, later used to represent the sun god Ra, was originally the symbol of Horus. Here two monumental falcons (opposite) guard an entrance to the Temple of Horus at Edfu.

The Sphinx at Gizeh, captured at the height of a son-et-lumière performance, is the most famous monument dedicated to Horus.

Heru-Behudti

One of the greatest and most important of all the forms of Horus is Heru-Behudti, who typifies midday, and therefore the greatest heat of the sun. It was in this form that Horus waged war against Set. His principal shrines were at Edfu, Philae, Mesen, Aat-ab, and Tanis, where he was worshipped under the form of a lion trampling upon its enemies. In general, however, he is depicted as hawk-headed and bearing in his hand a weapon, usually a club or mace, to symbolize his character as a destroyer. In the Arthurian romances we read of how certain knights, in combat with their enemies, grew stronger as the sun waxed in the heavens, and when its beams declined their strength failed them. As they grew in power, the solar heroes frequently became insane, and laid about them with such pitiless fury that they slaughtered thousands in a manner of which no ordinary warrior would be capable. This is typical of the strength and fury of the sun at midday in Eastern climates. Heru-Behudti, god of the midday sun, was the pitiless warrior wielding the club, perhaps typifying sunstroke, and the bow and arrows, symbolizing his fierce beams, which were to destroy the dragon of night and his fiendish crew. At midday he was all-conquering

In one of his most important forms as Heru-Behudti, symbol of the fierce heat of the sun at midday, Horus is normally portrayed as a lion. This lion relief is at Philae, a significant centre of the Heru-Behudti cult.

and had trampled the night-dragon out of sight. In this manner, too, he represented the force of good against that of evil.

In the myths of the battles of Horus it is easy to discern what is perhaps the most universal mythological conception – the solar myth. Horus (Heru-Behudti, that is Horus of Behudet, or Edfu) was originally a sun-god, and as such was equivalent to Ra, but in time the two gods came to be regarded as separate and distinct personages, Ra being the highest, and Horus serving him as a sort of war captain. The winged disk, therefore, represented the powers of light, while the wicked Set and his companions symbolized darkness. Thus it is that while Horus was always victorious over his enemies, he never succeeded (according to the most widespread form of the tradition) in destroying them utterly.

When Horus had routed the enemy in the form of a winged disk (see page 82), that symbol came to be regarded as an excellent protective against violence and destruction. It was therefore repeated many times – especially in the New Kingdom – in temples, on monuments, stelae, and so on. In its simplest form the image is merely that of a winged disk, but at times there is a serpent on either side of the disk, representing the goddesses Nekhbet and Uazet.

The principal version of the myth, dealing with Heru-Behudti, or Horus of Edfu, was really a local form belonging to Edfu, though in time it gained a wider acceptance. In other forms of the legend other gods took the chief role as destroyer of the enemies of Ra.

Fused with this legend of light and darkness was another that relates how Horus avenged the death of Osiris (see page 80).

It is noticeable that in this second myth there exists some confusion between Heru-Behudti (Horus the Elder) and Horus the Child, respectively brother and son of Osiris. No mention is made of Osiris in the Edfu text, but that this myth is a sequel to the legend of Osiris is implied by the circumstance that the defeated Set is handed over for punishment to Isis and Horus the Child.

In this legend one of the most noteworthy circumstances is that the followers of Horus were armed with weapons of metal. His followers are called in the Egyptian text *mesniu*, or *mesnitu*, which in all probability signifies "workers in metal" or "blacksmiths". The worshippers of Heru-Behudti continually alluded to him as "lord of the Forge-city" or Edfu, where tradition asserted he carried on the work of a blacksmith. At Edfu, indeed, the great golden disk of the sun itself had been forged, and in the temple of that city was a chamber behind the sanctuary called Mesnet, or "the foundry", where blacksmith priests attended upon the god. From sculptures upon the walls of the temple we see that these are arrayed in short robes and a species of collar which is almost a cape, that they carry their spears head downward, and a weapon of metal resembling a dagger. Heru-Behudti, who accompanies them, is dressed in a similar fashion, and is represented as spearing a hippopotamus, round which he has wound a double chain of metal.

Horus son of Isis and Osiris, or Horus the Child, was another important form of the god. He represented the rising sun, as did several other forms of Horus, and possessed many aspects or variants. His shrines were so numerous that at one epoch or another he was identified with all

Horus, in his familiar falcon-headed guise and wearing the twin crown of Upper and Lower Egypt, spears a hippopotamus. He is particularly associated with the city of Edfu, long a centre of metalworking and the forging of weapons.

Isis suckling the infant Horus while hidden amidst the reeds of the Delta to escape the wrath of Set. The two deities are attended by Thoth (left) and Amen-Ra, offering symbols of life.

the other Horus-gods, but he chiefly represented the new sun, born daily, and he was son and successor of Osiris. He was extremely popular, as being a well-marked type of resurrection after death. As Osiris represented "yesterday", so Horus, his son, stood for "today" in the Egyptian mind. Although some texts state that Osiris was his father, others claim this position for Ra, but the two in this instance are really one and the same. Osiris became the father of Horus after he was dead; such is the origin of several sun-heroes. The birth of such heroes is usually obscure. Isis, while tending the infant Horus and in fear of the persecutions of Set, took shelter in the swamps of the Delta, and hid herself and her child amidst a dense mass of papyrus plants. To the Egyptian of the Delta it would of course seem as if the sun took its rise from amidst the papyrus-covered swamps that stretched on every side to the horizon, so we may regard this part of the myth as allegory pure and simple.

The filial respect that Horus displayed for the memory of his father Osiris won him much honour from the Egyptians. He it was who fixed the details of the god's mummification, and who set the standard for the pious Egyptian son. In this respect he was regarded as a helper of the dead, and was thought to mediate between them and the judges of the Duat. In his work of caring for the deceased he had a number of helpers, known as the followers of Horus, who were regarded as gods of the cardinal points. They are given positions of great importance in the *Book of the Dead*, and shared the protection of the body of the deceased. They were four in number and were named Hapi, Tuamutef, Amset, and Qebhsennuf.

In certain texts Horus son of Isis and Osiris is represented as a child, with forefinger to lip, and wearing the lock of hair at the side of the head which indicates youth. In later times he was figured in a great many different fanciful forms.

SET

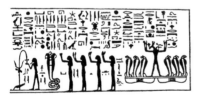

Set was linked with the autumn equinox, in which role he was perceived as stealing the light of the sun to shorten the days. In this illustration he appears on the right arranging the balance between day and night.

The cult of Set was of the greatest antiquity, and although in later times he was regarded as evil personified, this was not his original role. According to the priests of Heliopolis he was the son of Geb and Nut, and therefore brother of Osiris, Isis, and Nephthys, husband of the latter goddess and father of Anubis. These relationships, however, were all manufactured for him at a comparatively late period. In the Pyramid Texts we find Set acting as a friend to the dead, and he even assisted Osiris to reach heaven by means of a ladder. He is also associated with Horus and is regarded as his equal. But in time they came to be regarded as mortal enemies, who were only prevented from entirely destroying one another by the wise Thoth. Horus the Elder was the god of the sky by day, and Set the god of the sky by night. The one was in fact the direct opposite of the other.

The derivation of the name Set presents many difficulties of elucidation. The determinative of his hieroglyph is either the figure of an animal or a stone, which latter seems to symbolize the stony or desert country on either side of the Nile. The animal which pictorially represents him has not been identified, but various authorities have likened it to a

camel and an okapi. In any case it must have been a denizen of the desert inimical to man.

As Horus was the god of the North, so was Set god of the South. Brugsch considered Set symbolized the downward motion of the sun in the lower hemisphere, thus making him the source of the destructive heat of summer. As the days began to shorten and the nights to lengthen it was thought that he stole the light from the sun-god. He was likewise instrumental in the monthly destruction of the moon. Storms, earthquakes, and eclipses and all natural phenomena which caused darkness were attributed to him, and from an ethical point of view he was the god of sin and evil.

We find the myths of the combat between Set and Horus evolving from a simple opposition of day and night into a combat between the two gods (see page 80). Ra and Osiris, instead of Horus, are sometimes ranged against Set. The combat symbolized the moral idea of the victory of good over evil, and those of the dead who were justified were regarded as having overcome Set as Osiris had done. In his combat with the sun-god Set took the form of the monster serpent Apep and was accompanied by an army of lesser serpents and reptiles of every description. In later times we find him

The curious animal-head that distinguishes Set is normally interpreted as that of a camel, an animal ubiquitous in Egypt.

Though Horus and Set are normally considered as opponents, they are sometimes combined into a single deity.

identified with Typhon. All desert animals and those which inhabited the waters were regarded as the children of Set, as were animals with red hair or skins, or even red-haired men. Such animals were often sacrificed ritually in propitiation of Set. In the month of Pachons an antelope and a black pig were sacrificed to him in order to deter him from attacking the full moon, and on the great festival of Heru-Behudti such birds and fish as were thought to be of his following were trodden underfoot to the cry that Ra had triumphed over his enemies.

Set had also a kingdom in the northern sky, and his peculiar abode was the Great Bear. As in some other countries, the north was considered by the Egyptians as the place of darkness, cold, and death.

The goddess Reret, who has the head and body of a hippopotamus, was supposed to have the evil influence of Set in restraint. She is pictured as holding darkness fettered by a chain, and is considered to be a form of Isis.

It was probably around the time of the Twenty-second Dynasty that the worship of Set began to decline, and that he took on the shape of an evil deity. The theory has been put forward that the Hyksos invaders identified him with certain of their gods, and that this sufficed to bring him into disrepute with the Egyptians.

NEPHTHYS

Nephthys, the female counterpart of the evil Set, was nevertheless closely associated with her sister Isis, and was considered by Plutarch to have conceived Anubis illicitly with Osiris. Here the thrones of Isis, Osiris and Nephthys are being bound together by Horus and Thoth.

The female counterpart of Set was Nephthys. She was the daughter of Geb and Nut, the sister and wife of Set, and the mother of Anubis, but whether by Osiris or Set is not clear. The words Nebt-het mean "the lady of the house", or sky. Although Nephthys is associated with Set, she appears to remain more faithful to her sister Isis, whom she assists to regain the scattered limbs of Osiris. She is represented in the form of a woman wearing upon her head the symbol of her name, that is a basket and a house (reading Nebt-het). She appears in some ways in the *Book of the Dead* as an assistant of her sister Isis, standing behind Osiris when the hearts of the dead are weighed, and kneeling at the head of Osiris' bier. She was supposed to possess great magical powers like her sister, and resembles her in possessing many forms. She is also supposed to protect Osiris in his form of moon-god.

Plutarch throws some light upon Egyptian belief concerning this goddess. He says that Anubis was the son of Osiris and Nephthys, and that Set was first apprised of their amour by finding a garland of flowers that had been left behind him by Osiris. As Isis represents fruitfulness, so, he says, Nephthys signifies corruption. Budge, commenting upon this passage, says that it is clear that Nephthys is the personification of darkness and of all that belongs to it, and that her attributes were of a passive rather than of an active character. "She was the opposite of Isis in every respect. Isis symbolized birth, growth, development, and vigour; but Nephthys was the type of death, decay, diminution, and immobility. The two goddesses were, however, associated inseparably with each other." Isis, according to Plutarch, represents the part of the world that is visible, whilst Nephthys represents that which is invisible.

Isis and Nephthys represent respectively the things which already exist and the things that are yet to come into being, the beginning and the end, birth and death, and life and death.

We have unfortunately no means of knowing what the original conception of the attributes of Nephthys was, but it is most improbable that it included any of the views on the subject that were current in Plutarch's time. Nephthys is not a goddess with well-defined characteristics, but she may, generally speaking, be described as, "the goddess of the death which is not eternal." Budge says that Nephthys, although a goddess of death, was associated with the coming into existence of the life which springs from death. With Isis she prepared the funeral bed of Osiris and made his mummy wrappings. Along with Isis she guarded the corpse of Osiris. In later times the goddesses were represented by two priestesses whose hair was shaved off and who wore ram's-wool garlands upon their heads. On the arm of one was a fillet inscribed to Isis, and the other wore a like band inscribed to Nephthys.

Nephthys and Isis sit at the head and foot respectively of the bier while Anubis and the frog-goddess Heqet reconstitute the body of Osiris, under the guidance of Thoth.

ANUBIS

Anubis, or, as the Egyptians called him, An-pu, was according to some the son of Osiris and Nephthys, and to others the son of Set. He had the head of a jackal and the body of a man, and was evidently symbolic of that

Three Anubis figures from a painting in the tomb of the artisan Inherkha at Deir el-Medina, Luxor.

animal, which prowled about the tombs of the dead. His worship was of great antiquity, and he was the guide of the dead in the underworld on their way to the abode of Osiris.

In many mythologies a dog is the companion of the dead man to the other world. Its remains are found in prehistoric graves; in both Mexico and Peru dogs were sacrificed at burial, and, indeed, the custom is a very widespread one. Now it is not improbable that Anubis may have typified the prehistoric half-domesticated jackal, or early type of dog.

Anubis was particularly worshipped at Lycopolis and at Abt. He plays a prominent part in the *Book of the Dead*, especially in those passages which are connected with the justification and the embalming of the deceased. It was he who embalmed the body of Osiris. Indeed, he rendered great assistance to the god's mourning sisters, and in this he may typify the faithful and helpful qualities of the dog. This is all the more striking if he is to be accepted as the son of Set, and the whole evolution of the deity would seem to imply that whereas the semi-savage, half-domesticated dog was originally nocturnal and of doubtful value, under domestication its virtues became apparent. It is probable that, could research be pushed back to a sufficiently remote epoch, and did paintings of such an early period exist, we should find Anubis pictured as the faithful dog preceding the deceased on the journey to the Duat. Later, when every deity in the picture had evolved to fulfil a special function, and perhaps in an area where the jackal or dog was totemic, we find the companion of the dead still accompanying him, indeed, still his guide through the darkness, but in the guise and with the attributes of a full-grown deity. How he came to be the mummifier of Osiris it is hard to say; probably the association of the jackal with the burial-ground would account for this. He was symbolic of the grave.

A speech of Anubis in the *Book of the Dead*, chapter 151, is suggestive of his protective character. "I have come," he says, "to protect Osiris." In many countries the dog is dispatched with the deceased for the purpose of protecting him against various grisly enemies he may meet on the way to the Kingdom of Osiris, and it is not unlikely that Anubis played a similar part in very early times.

It is the duty of Anubis to see that the beam of the great balance in which the heart of the deceased is weighed is in its proper position. As Thoth acts for the gods, so Anubis appears for the dead man, whom he also protects against the "Eater of the Dead". He also guided the souls of the dead through the underworld, being assisted in this duty by Up-uaut, another jackal-headed deity, whose name signifies "Opener of the Ways". These gods have sometimes been confused, but in certain texts they are separately alluded to. The name of the latter deity is significant of his probable early function. Anubis, thinks Dr Budge, was the opener of the roads of the north, and Up-uaut of those of the south. "In fact," he says, "Anubis was the personification of the summer solstice, and Ap-uat [Up-uaut] of the winter solstice." He goes on to say that when they appear with the two Utchats, or eyes of Ra, they symbolize the four quarters of heaven and of earth, and the four seasons of the year.

At Heliopolis, Anubis was to some extent fused with Horus as regards his attributes, and in some manner he took on the character of the old fusion between Horus and Set, in this latter connection personifying death and

Anubis plays a major role in the *Book of the Dead*, particularly as the divine embalmer and an expert in mummification. His jackal head may derive from the frequent presence of jackals around Egyptian cemeteries.

decay. In the *Golden Ass* of Apuleius we find that Anubis had votaries in Rome, and it is noticeable that in this account he is spoken of as having a dog's head.

THOTH

Thoth, or Tehuti, was a highly composite deity. His birth was coeval with that of Ra. He is alluded to as the counter of the stars, the measurer and enumerator of the earth, as being twice great and thrice great lord of books, scribe of the gods, and as possessing knowledge of divine speech, in which he was "mighty". In general he was figured in human form with the head of an ibis, but sometimes he appears in the shape of that bird. He wears upon his head the crescent moon and disk, the Atef crown, and the crowns of the North and South. In the *Book of the Dead* he is drawn as holding the writing reed and palette of the scribe, and as placing on his tablets the records of the deceased whose heart is being weighed before him.

There is no reason to suppose that Thoth was totemic in character, as he belongs to the cosmogonic or nature deities, few or none of whom were of this type. Another form of Thoth is that of a baboon, which, it has been stated, symbolizes his powers of equilibrium.

Thoth in his typical form as a human with the head of an ibis, wearing on his head the crescent moon and the disk of the full moon. He was the god of books, measurements and all mental activities.

Thoth also took the shape of a baboon. This is how he appears in a statue at Ashmunein, a village that became an important religious centre devoted to his cult.

The remains of a Hellenic temple at Hermopolis. Hermopolis was the Greek name for Ashmunein, and worship of Thoth there continued into Hellenic times under his Greek name, Hermes.

Thoth as a baboon supervises the weighing of the heart of the deceased before Osiris, reproduced from the ancient Papyrus of Nebseni.

His principal seat of worship was Hermopolis, where Ra was supposed to have risen for the first time. To Thoth was ascribed the mental powers of Ra, and, indeed, the dicta of Ra seem to have come from his lips. He was the Divine Speech personified. But we are looking ahead. Let us discover his primitive significance before we enumerate the more or less complex attributes that were heaped upon him in later times.

It is pretty clear that Thoth is originally a moon god. He is called the "great god" and "lord of heaven". In early cosmologies the moon is the great regulator of the seasons, hence the expressions "seed moon", the "deer moon", the "grain" or "harvest moon", and so on. A lunar calendar is invariably in use prior to the introduction of the computation of time by solar revolution. The moon is thus the "great measurer", and Thoth was a measurer because he was a moon-god. As Aah-Tehuti he symbolizes the new moon, as it is from the first appearance of the moon that time is measured. His eye signifies the full moon in the same manner that the eye of Ra signifies the sun at mid-day. But it also symbolizes the left eye of Ra, or the cold half of the year, when the sun's rays are not so strong. It is sometimes also called the "black eye of Horus", the "white eye" being the sun. This serves to illustrate how greatly the attributes of the Egyptian deities had become confused. As he was a moon-god, so he was to some extent connected with moisture, and we find him alluded to in chapter 95 of the *Book of the Dead* as a rain and thunder god.

Thoth as Soul-Recorder

It is, however, as the recorder of souls before Osiris that Thoth was important in the eyes of the Egyptian priesthood. He held this office because of his knowledge of letters and his gift of knowing what was right or in equilibrium. Again, he had the power of imparting the manner in which words should be correctly spoken. The mode of speech, the tone in which words were pronounced, spelt success or failure in both prayer and magical incantations. The secret of this Thoth taught to men, and this it was that the Egyptians especially desired to learn. Through the formula of Thoth the gates of the Duat were opened to the deceased, and he or she was safeguarded against its terrors. The *Book of the Dead* was indeed believed to be the "Book of Thoth", as was the *Book of Breathings*, a much later work. The Greek writers upon things Egyptian imagined Thoth, whom they called Hermes Trismegistos, or Thrice Great, as the prime source of all learning and wisdom. They ascribed to him the invention of the sciences of astronomy and astrology, mathematics, geometry, and medicine. The letters of the alphabet were also his invention, from which sprang the subsequent arts of reading and writing.

MAAT

The goddess Maat closely resembles Thoth, and has indeed been regarded as the female counterpart of that god. She was one of the original goddesses, for when the boat of Ra rose above the waters of the primeval abyss of Nu for the first time, she had her place in it beside Thoth. She is symbolized by the ostrich feather, which she either holds or which decorates her headdress: it is likely that the equal-sidedness of the feather, its division into halves, rendered it a fitting symbol of balance or equilibrium. The name Maat indicates "that which is straight". Among the ancient Egyptians it came to imply anything that was true, genuine, or real. Thus the goddess was the personification of law, order, and truth. She indicated the regularity with which Ra rose and set in the sky, and, assisted by Thoth, wrote down his daily course for him every day. In this capacity she is called the "daughter of Ra" and the "Eye of Ra". As the personification of justice her moral power was immense and inexorable. In fact, she came to be regarded as that fate from whom every man receives his just deserts. She sat in a hall in the underworld to hear the confessions of the dead, the door of which was guarded by Anubis. The deceased had to satisfy forty-two assessors or judges in this hall, after which they proceeded to the presence of Osiris, whom they assured that they had "done Maat", and that they had been purified by her.

The goddess Maat is the personification of order, truth and justice, concepts so highly regarded in the well-ordered society of Egypt.

RA

Ra, the great god of the sun, appears to have occupied a prominent position in the Egyptian pantheon from a very early period. The Egyptians of later days appear to have thought that the name was in some way associated with creation. Sun-worship in Egypt was very ancient, and it is probable that a number of sun-cults became fused into that of Ra. It is certain, indeed, that this was the case with the cult of the hawk god Heru or Horus. Both of these deities are usually figured with the body of a man and the head of a hawk,

but they sometimes have the veritable form of that bird. The hawk in Egypt appears to have been identified with the sun from the earliest times. Its power of sight and the heights to which it can rise were probably the reasons for its association with the great luminary of day. But in many lands birds of heaven aspiring flight have symbolized the sun. It is strange that just as we find the bird and the serpent combined in the Mexican god Quetzalcoatl, so we discover them to some extent associated in Ra, who wears as his symbol the disk of the sun encircled by the serpent Khut.

The Egyptians had several varying conceptions as to the manner in which the sun crossed the heavens. One of these was that it sailed over the watery mass of the sky in relays of boats or barques. Thus the rising sun occupied the barque Manzet, which means "growing strong", and the evening sun was ferried to the place of setting by the barque Mesektet, which means "growing weak", both being allegorical titles for the rising and setting sun. The definite path of Ra across the sky had been planned at the time of creation by the goddess Maat, who personified justice and order.

The daily voyage of Ra was assisted by a company of friendly deities, who navigated his barque to the place of the setting sun, the course being set out by Thoth and Maat, while Horus acted as steersman and commander. On each side of the boat swam one of two pilot fishes called Abtu and Ant, but, notwithstanding the assistance of his fellow deities, the barque of Ra was constantly beset by the most grisly monsters and demons, who strove to put every obstacle in the way of its successful passage.

By far the most potent of these was the serpent Apep, who personified the darkness of night, and concerning whom we gain much information from the *Book of Overthrowing Apep*, which gives spells and other

The sun god Ra (opposite left) represented by the hawk's head frequently used to indicate Horus, in a relief from the temple of Sobek, the crocodile god, at Kom Ombo. He is identified by the sun-disk on his head.

A solar boat of Ra, one of several in which the sun was considered to cross the sky, from a wall painting at Abydos.

The hawk-headed Ra wearing on his head the disk of the sun encircled by the serpent Khut. The cult of Ra gradually declined as Osiris acquired many of his attributes.

instructions for the checkmating of the monster, which were recited daily in the temple of Amen-Ra at Thebes. In these Apep is referred to as a crocodile and a serpent, and it is described how by the aid of sympathetic magic he is to be speared, cut with knives, decapitated, roasted, and finally consumed by fire, and his evil followers also. These magical acts were duly carried out at Thebes day by day, and it was supposed that they greatly assisted the journey of the sun-god.

Primitive as is the nature of sun-worship, it possesses elements that enable it to survive where many more advanced and complicated cults succumb. To the peasants of Egypt the sun would, it might be thought, appear as the god par excellence, the great quickener and fructifier; but we find the cult of Ra more or less of an aristocratic theological system, in early times at least; and for the cult of the people we have to turn to the worship of Osiris. This is confirmed by the Egyptian belief that the paradise of Ra was a sphere more spiritual by far than that of Osiris, with its purely material delights. Those happy enough to gain the heaven of the sun-god were clothed with light, and their food was also described as "light". The Osirian paradise, by contrast, consisted of converse with Osiris and feasting with him. As the Egyptian mind was of a strongly material cast, it greatly favoured the conception a "field of reeds" and a "field of peace", where humans could enjoy the good things and creature-comforts that they so much desired upon earth, rather than the unsubstantial sphere of Ra.

Ra and Osiris

A great struggle was waged for many centuries between the priesthoods of Ra and Osiris, but in the end the beliefs clustering around the latter deity gained pre-eminence, and he took over the titles, powers, and attributes of the great god of the sun. Then it was probable that the conception of a moon- and a sun-god became fused in his person. The worship of Osiris was fundamentally African and Egyptian in character, but there is strong reason to believe that the cult of Ra possessed many foreign elements, possibly West Asiatic in origin, which may account for the apparent coldness with which the masses of Egypt regarded his worship. Heliopolis, his city, contained many inhabitants of Asiatic birth, and this may account to some extent for the introduction of some of the tenets in his creed which the native Egyptians found unpalatable.

The souls of Ra (left) and Osiris meeting in Busiris, a detail reproduced from the Papyrus of Ani.

There is no doubt, however, that to the aristocracy of Egypt at least, Ra stood in the position of creator and father of the gods. Osiris stood in relation to him as a son. In fact, the relations of these two deities may be regarded as that between the Christian God the Father and God the Son, and just as in certain theologies the figure of the son has overshadowed that of the father so did Osiris overshadow Ra.

The god Tem, or Atum, originally the local deity of Heliopolis, was in the dynastic period held to be one of the forms of Ra, and a personification of the setting sun. Tem was one of the first gods of the Egyptians. He is depicted as sailing in the boat of Ra, with whom he was clearly united in early times as Ra-Tem. He appears to have been a god who possessed many attributes in common with Ra, and later on he seems to have been identified with Osiris as well. In the myth of Ra and Isis, Ra says, "I am Khepra in the morning, and Ra at noonday, and Tem in the evening," which shows that to the Egyptians the day was divided into three parts each of which was presided over by a special form of the sun god. Tem was worshipped in one of his forms as a serpent, a fairly common shape for a sun-god, for in many countries the snake or serpent, tail in mouth, symbolizes the disk of the sun.

The god Tem, or Atum, wearing the double crown of Upper and Lower Egypt, seated within the solar disk in a solar boat. Tem was an ancient sun god of Heliopolis, associated particularly with the sunset.

The Sacred Beetle

Khepra, the remaining form of Ra, is generally represented in human form with a beetle upon his head. The worship of the beetle was time-honoured in Egypt, and we must regard its fusion with the cult of Ra as due to priestly influence. The scarabaeus, having laid its eggs in the sand of Egypt, rolls them into a little ball of manure, which it then propels across the sand with its hind legs to a hole that it has previously dug, where the eggs are hatched by the rays of the sun. This action of the beetle seemed to the ancient Egyptians to resemble the rolling of the sun across the heavens so that Khepra, the rising luminary, was symbolized by it. Khepra is a deity of some importance, for he is called creator of the gods and father of the gods. He was also looked upon as a type of the resurrection because of his

The sun god in the underworld, with the beetle Khepra at his head. Khepra was thought to signify the rising sun.

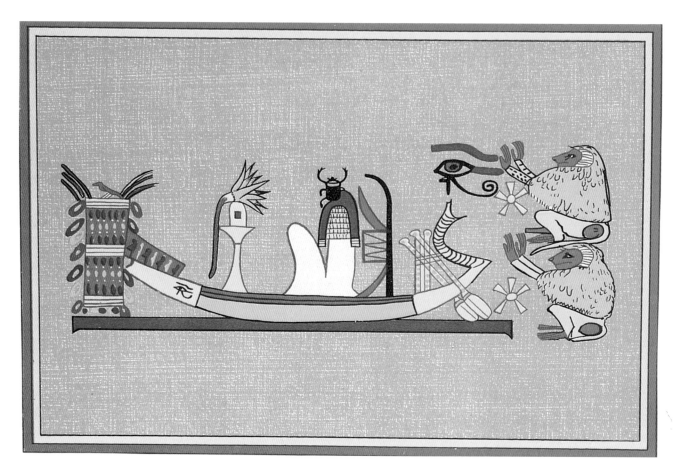

The sacred beetle Khepra seated in a solar boat. Khepra was considered to be another form of Ra, perhaps because the scarab beetle's action of rolling a ball of dung across the sand recalled the movement of the sun across the sky.

symbolizing the ball enclosing living germs, and probably in a secondary sense, because the rising sun steps as it were from the grave of night morning after morning with the greatest certainty. The scarabs which were found on Egyptian mummies typified this hope of resurrection, and have been found in Egyptian tombs as old as the time of the Fourth Dynasty.

AMEN

Although the god Amen appears to have been numbered among the deities of Egypt as early as the Fifth Dynasty, when he was alluded to as one of the primeval gods, it was not until a later period that his votaries began to exercise the enormous power which they finally wielded throughout Egypt. With the exception of Ra and Osiris, the worship of Amen was more widespread than that of any other god in the Nile valley; but the circumstances behind the growth of his cult certainly point to its having been disseminated by political rather than religious propaganda.

What his attributes were in the time of the Ancient Empire we do not know. The name means "what is hidden", or what cannot be seen, and we are constantly informed in votive hymns and other compositions that he is "hidden to his children" and "hidden to gods and men". It has been advanced that these expressions refer to the setting of the sun, but there is far better reason for supposing that they imply that Amen is a god who cannot be viewed by mortal eyes, invisible and inscrutable. It is not difficult to see that the conception of such a deity would speedily win favour with a priestly and theological class, who might strain after a form of godhead less

crude than the purely symbolic systems that held sway in the country. In fact, the whole theological history of Amen seems that of a priesthood determined to impose upon a rather materialistic population a more spiritual type of worship.

Amen was represented in numerous forms: in the shape of a man seated on a throne, with the head of a frog and the body of a man, with a serpent's head, as an ape and as a lion. But the most general form in which he was drawn was that of a bearded man wearing on his head two long and very straight plumes, which are coloured alternately red and green or red and blue. He is clothed in a linen tunic, wears bracelets, and necklet, and from the back of his dress there hangs an animal's tail, which denotes that he was a god originating in early times. In a later form he has the head of a hawk when fused with Ra.

The great centre of his worship and of his rise to power was the city of Thebes where, in the Twelfth Dynasty a temple was built in his honour. At that period he was a mere local god, but when the princes of Thebes came to power throughout Egypt the reputation of Amen rose with theirs and he became a prominent god in Upper Egypt. His priesthood, seizing upon the new political conditions, succeeded in identifying him with Ra and his subsidiary forms, all of whose attributes they ascribed to Amen; but they

The god Amen (centre), depicted on a relief from the entrance pylon to the temple of Khonsu at Karnak. Amen was the most widely worshipped Egyptian god after Ra and Osiris.

Amen in his most common form as a bearded man wearing his unmistakable headdress with two tall, straight plumes coloured with red, green and blue.

further stated that although their deity included in himself all their characteristics, he was much greater and loftier than they. As we have already observed, the god of the capital of Egypt for the time being was the national deity, and when this lot fell to the fortune of Amen his priesthood took full advantage of it. When the Hyksos overran the country, Amen, thanks to his priestly protagonists, weathered the storm and, because of internecine strife, had become the god par excellence of the Egyptians. When the country recovered from its troubles and matters began to right themselves once more, the military successes of the kings of the Eighteenth Dynasty redounded greatly to the power and glory of Amen, and the spoil of conquered Palestine and Syria loaded his temples.

Osiris, as the popular god, could not well be displaced, as he had too large a hold on the imagination of the people, and his cult and character were of too peculiar a nature to concede to usurpation by another deity. But the cult of Ra was challenged directly by that of Amen, a deity who not only presented like attributes, but whose worship was on the whole more spiritual than that of the great sun-god. We do not know what theological battles were waged over the question of the supremacy of the two gods, but we do know that a fusion of the gods took place. It would be rash to assert that this amalgamation was a planned affair between the two warring cults, and it is more probable that their devotees quietly acquiesced in a gradual process of fusion.

Amen's Rise to Power

Many hymns of Amen-Ra, especially the one occurring in the papyrus of Hu-nefer, show the completeness of this fusion and the rapidity with which Amen had risen to power. In about a century from being a mere local god he had gained the title of "king of the gods" of Egypt. His priesthood had become by far the most powerful and wealthy in the land, and even rivalled royalty itself. The political power of his priests can only be described as enormous. They made war and peace, and when the Ramessid Dynasty came to an end the high-priest of Amen-Ra was raised to the royal power, instituting the Twenty-first Dynasty, or "dynasty of priest-kings". But they could not enforce the payment of tribute which their predecessors had wrung from the surrounding countries and their poverty increased rapidly. The shrines of the god languished for want of attendants, and even the higher ranks of the priesthood itself suffered a good deal of hardship. Robber bands infested the vicinity of the temples, and many of the royal tombs were looted.

But if their power waned, their pretensions certainly did not, and even in the face of Libyan aggression in the Delta they continued to vaunt the glory of the god whom they served. Examining the texts and hymns of Amen-Ra, we find that he was considered the creator of the universe, the "unknown god". All the attributes of the entire Egyptian pantheon were lavished upon him, with the exception of those of Osiris; the priests of Amen-Ra could not displace the great god of the dead. In one of his forms, certainly, that of Khensu the Moon-god, Amen bears a slight likeness to Osiris, but we cannot say that in this form he usurps the role of the god of the underworld in any respect.

The great temple of Amen at Karnak, (opposite), with the sacred lake in the foreground. This huge temple complex was built over a period of more than one thousand years.

Amen-Ra even occupied the shrines of many other gods throughout the Nile valley, absorbing their attributes and entirely taking their place. One of his most popular forms was that of a goose, and the animal was sacred to him in many parts of Egypt, as was the ram.

Small figures of him made in the Ptolemaic form have the bearded face of a man, the body of a beetle, the wings of a hawk, human legs with the toes and claws of a lion. The entire pesedt or company of gods was supposed to be unified in Amen, and indeed we may describe his cult as one of the most serious attempts of antiquity to formulate a system of monotheism.

The Oracle of Jupiter-Ammon

No part of Egypt was free from the dominion of Amen-Ra, which spread north and south, east and west, and had ramifications in Syria, Nubia, and other Egyptian dependencies. Its most powerful centres were Thebes, Hermonthis, Coptos, Panopolis, Hermopolis Magna, and in Lower Egypt, Memphis, Sais, Heliopolis, and Mendes. In one of the oases in later times he had a great oracle, known as that of Jupiter-Ammon, a mysterious spot frequented by Greeks and Romans, who went there to consult the deity. Here every roguery of priestcraft was practised. An idol of the god was on occasion carried through the temple by his priests, responding, if he were in a good humour, to his votaries, not by speech, but by nodding and pointing with outstretched arm. (We know from Classical authors that the Egyptians possessed the most wonderful skill in the manufacture of automata, and there is every reason to believe that the god responded to the questions of the eager devotees by mechanical means.) Even Alexander the Great paid a visit to this famous shrine, as did Lysander and Hannibal.

MUT

The great female counterpart of Amen-Ra was Mut, the "world-mother". She is usually represented as a woman wearing the united crowns of north and south, and holding the papyrus sceptre. In some pictures she is shown with wings, and in others the heads of vultures project from her shoulders. Like her husband, she is occasionally adorned with every description of attribute, human and animal, probably to typify her universal nature. Mut, like Amen, swallowed up a great many of the attributes of the female deities of Egypt. She was thus identified with Bast, Nekhbet, and others. Even Hathor was identified with her, as was Ta-urt and every other goddess who could be regarded as having the attributes of a mother. Her worship centred at Thebes, where her temple was situated a little to the south of the shrine of Amen-Ra. She was styled the "lady of heaven" and "queen of the gods", and her hieroglyphic symbol, a vulture, was worn on the crowns of Egypt's queens. The temple of Mut at Thebes was built by Amen-hetep III about 1450 BC. Its approach was lined by a wonderful avenue of sphinxes, and it overlooked an artificial lake. Mut was probably the original female counterpart of Nu, who in some manner became associated with Amen. She is mentioned only once in the *Book of the Dead* in the Theban Recension, which is not a little strange considering the reputation she must have enjoyed with the priesthood of Amen.

Amen continued to be worshipped in Greek and Roman times, and his famous oracle, Jupiter-Ammon at Siwa Oasis, was consulted by Alexander the Great and Hannibal, among others.

PTAH

A sphinx from the avenue leading to the temple of Mut at Luxor, part of the complex generally referred to as Thebes by the Greeks.

Ptah was the greatest of the gods of Memphis. He personified the rising sun, or rather, a phase of it – that is, he represented the orb at the time when it begins to rise above the horizon, or immediately after it has risen. Brugsch suggests that the name means "sculptor" or "engraver", and as Ptah was the god of all handicrafts it seems probable that this is correct. Ptah seems to have retained the same characteristics from the period of the Second

A wall relief of Ptah,
showing the god in his usual
guise as a mummified man.

Dynasty down to the latest times. In early days he seems to have been regarded as a creator, or perhaps he was confounded with one of the first Egyptian creative deities. We find him alluded to in the Pyramid Text of Teta as the owner of a "workshop", and the passage seems to imply that it was Ptah who fashioned new boats in which the souls of the dead were to live in the Duat. From the *Book of the Dead* we learn that he was a great worker in metals, a master architect, and framer of everything in the universe; and the fact that the Romans identified him with Vulcan greatly assists our understanding of his attributes.

It was Ptah who, in company with Khnemu, carried out the commands of Thoth concerning the creation of the universe. To Khnemu was given the fashioning of animals, while Ptah was employed in making the heavens and the earth. The great metal plate which was supposed to form the floor of heaven and the roof of the sky was made by Ptah, who also framed the supports which upheld it. We find him constantly associated with other gods – that is, he takes on the attributes or characteristics of other deities for certain fixed purposes. For example, as architect of the universe he partakes of the nature of Thoth.

Ptah is usually represented as a bearded man with a bald head, dressed in habiliments which fit as closely as a shroud. From the back of his neck hangs a menat, the symbol of happiness, and along with the usual insignia of royalty and godhead he holds the symbol of stability. As Ptah-Seker he represents the union of the creative power with that of chaos or darkness: Ptah-Seker is, indeed, a form of Osiris in his guise of the Night-sun, or dead Sun-god. Seker is figured as a hawk-headed man in the form of a mummy, his body resembling that of Ptah.

Ptah shaping the egg of the world
on his potter's wheel.
His association with handicrafts
led naturally to his recognition as
the creator of the universe.

The Seker-boat

In the great ceremonies connected with this god, and especially on the day of his festival, a boat called the Seker-boat was placed upon a sledge at sunrise, at the time when the rays of the sun were slowly beginning to diffuse themselves over the earth. It was then drawn round the sanctuary, which act typified the revolution of the sun. This boat was known as Henu, and is mentioned several times in the *Book of the Dead*. It did not resemble an ordinary boat, but one end of it was much higher than the other, and was fashioned in the shape of the head of an animal resembling a gazelle. In the centre of the vessel was a coffer surmounted by a hawk with outspread wings, which was supposed to contain the body of Osiris, or of the dead sun-god. The Seker- or Henu-boat was probably a form of the Mesektet-boat, in which the sun sailed over the sky during the second half of his daily journey, and in which he entered the underworld in the evening. Although Seker was fairly popular as a deity in ancient Egypt, his attributes seem to have been entirely usurped by Ptah. We also find the triple-named deity Ptah-Seker-Asar or Ptah-Seker-Osiris, who is often represented as a hawk on coffers and sarcophagi. About the time of the Twenty-second Dynasty this triad had practically become one with Osiris. He has been described as the "triune god of the resurrection". There is very little doubt that the amalgamation of these gods was brought about by priestly influence.

Ptah was also connected with the god known as Tenen, who is usually

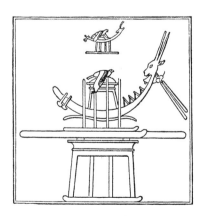

The Seker-boat, used in the ceremonies
connected with the Ptah-Seker-Osiris
deity, illustrated here on its sledge.

represented in human form and wearing on his head the crown with ostrich feathers. He is also drawn working at a potter's wheel, upon which he shapes the egg of the world. In other drawings he is depicted as holding a scimitar, with which he has carved out the earth. Tenen was thus probably a primeval creation god, and for that reason was coordinated with Ptah.

BAST

Bast, the Bubastis of the Greeks, possessed the attributes of the cat or lioness, the latter being a later development of her character. The name implies the "cutter" or "tearer", and she is also entitled "the lady of Sept" – that is, of the star Sothis. She was sometimes further identified with Isis and Hathor. In contradistinction to the fierce Sekhmet, she typified the mild fertilizing heat of the sun. The cat loves to bask in the sun's rays, and it is probably for this reason that the animal was taken as symbolizing this goddess. She is amalgamated with Sekhmet and Ra in a deity known as Sekhmet-Bast-Ra, and as such is represented as a woman with a man's head, and wings sprouting from her arms, and the heads of two vultures springing from her neck. She has also the claws of a lion.

She was the goddess of the eastern part of the Delta, and was worshipped at Bubastis, in Lower Egypt. Her worship seems to have been of very considerable antiquity in that region, and although she is mentioned in the Pyramid Texts, it is only occasionally that she figures in the *Book of the Dead*. In all probability she was originally a cat totem, and in any case was first worshipped in the shape of a cat pure and simple. Although she is connected with fire and with the sun, it would appear that she also has some association with the lunar disk, for her son Khonsu is a moon-god. Cat-gods are often associated with the moon.

The Festival of Bast

Herodotus gives a very picturesque description of a festival of this goddess which took place in the months of April and May. He says that the inhabitants of the city of Bubastis sailed toward it in ships, playing upon drums and tabors and making a great noise, those who did not play clapping their hands and singing loudly. Having arrived at the city, they danced and celebrated with drinking and song.

The goddess Bast, shown with her
characteristic lioness head,
was worshipped at Bubastis
in Lower Egypt. Large numbers
of mummified cats, associated
with the goddess, have been
found in that area.

Many images of Egyptian merry-making
have survived, including these
illustrations demonstrating individual
dance steps.

KHNEMU

At the city of Elephantine or Abu a great triad of gods was held in reverence. This consisted of Khnemu, Satet, and Anqet. The worship of the first was of great antiquity. His position had always been an exalted one, and even to the last he appears to have been of importance in the eyes of the Gnostics. Khnemu was probably a god of the pre-dynastic Egyptians. He was symbolized by the flat-horned ram, which appears to have been introduced into the country from the East. He is usually represented in the form of a ram-headed man wearing the white crown, and sometimes the disk. In some instances he is pictured as pouring water over the earth, and in others with a jug above his horns – a sure indication that he is connected in some way with moisture. His name signifies the builder or framer, and he it was who fashioned the first man upon a potter's wheel, who made the first egg from which sprang the sun, who made the bodies of the gods, and who continued to build them up and maintain them.

Khnemu had been worshipped at Elephantine from time immemorial and was therefore the god of the First Cataract. His female counterparts, Satet and Anqet, have been identified as a form of the star Sept and as a local Nubian goddess. From the texts it is pretty clear that Khnemu was originally a river-god who, like Hapi, was regarded as the god of the Nile and of the annual Nile flood, and it may be that he and Hapi were Nile gods introduced by two separate races, or by the people of two different portions of the country. In the texts he is alluded to as "father of the fathers of the gods and goddesses, lord of created things from himself, maker of heaven and earth and the Duat and water and mountains," so we see that, like Hapi, he had been identified with the creative deities. He is sometimes represented as having four rams' heads upon a human body, and as he united within himself the attributes of Ra, Shu, Geb, and Osiris, these heads may have typified the deities in question. Brugsch considered, however, that they symbolized the four elements – fire, air, earth, and water. But it is a little difficult to see how this could be so. In any case, when represented with four heads Khnemu typified the great primeval creative force.

An aerial view of the Nile, which creates a bright stripe of green, fertile land through the Egyptian desert.

HATHOR

It is no easy matter to gauge the true mythological significance of the Egyptian goddess Hathor, patron of women, of love, and of pleasure, Lady of Heaven, and Mistress of the Underworld. She occupied a very important position in the pantheon of ancient Egypt, dating from archaic times. We find a multitude of mythological ideas fused in Hathor: she is a moon-goddess, a sky-goddess, a goddess of the east, a goddess of the west, a cosmic deity, an agricultural goddess, a goddess of moisture, even on occasion a solar deity. Though her original status is thus somewhat obscure, it can be assumed that she is primarily a moon goddess, for reasons that are detailed below.

Evening tranquillity on Elephantine Island (opposite), a major centre for the worship of Khnemu, the ram-headed god of the Nile caratacts.

Hathor, goddess of women, love and pleasure, was originally worshipped in the form of a cow, as in this illustration from the Papyrus of Ani. In later representations she retained a headdress resembling the cow's horns with a lunar disk between them.

The original form in which Hathor was worshipped was that of a cow. Later she is represented as a woman with the head of a cow, and finally with a human head, the face broad, kindly, placid, and decidedly bovine, sometimes retaining the ears or horns of the animal she represents. She is also shown with a head-dress resembling a pair of horns with the moon-disk between them. Sometimes she is found in the form of a cow standing in a boat, surrounded by tall papyrus reeds. In mythology the cow is often identified with the moon, perhaps because of the horned appearance of the moon at certain seasons. The fact that Hathor the cow is sometimes shown in a boat suggests that she was also a water goddess, and heightens the probability that she was identified with the moon, for the latter was regarded by the Egyptians as the source of all moisture.

The name Hathor signifies "House of Horus" – that is, the sky – and there is no doubt that at one time Hathor was regarded as a sky-goddess, or a goddess of the eastern sky, where Horus was born; she has also been

A caretaker at the entrance to the temple of Hathor at Abu Simbel. Inside the sanctuary a statue of Hathor as a cow protects a further statue of the pharaoh Ramesses II.

identified with the night sky and with the sunset sky. If, however, we regard her as a moon-goddess, a good deal of the mythology concerning her will become clear. She is, for example, frequently spoken of as the "Eye of Ra", Ra, the sun-god, probably possessing in this instance the wider significance of sky-god. She is also designated "The Golden One", who stands high in the south as the Lady of Teka, and illuminates the west as the Lady of Sais. That she is mistress of the underworld is likewise not surprising when we consider her as identical with the moon, for does not the moon make a daily pilgrimage through Amentet? Neither is it astonishing that a goddess of moisture and vegetation should be found in the underworld dispensing water to the souls of the dead from the branches of a palm or a sycamore.

The temple of Hathor at Abu Simbel, which was painstakingly moved and reassembled on higher ground in 1968 with the construction of the High Dam at Aswan. Built by Ramesses II for his wife Nefertari, its entrance includes four 10-metre statues of the pharaoh and two of his wife.

Hathor as Love-Goddess

Though Hathor was specifically the goddess of love, other goddesses were considered to share some of her propensities: here Tuthmosis III is embraced by the protective scorpion goddess Selket, in a modern reproduction of an Egyptian original.

On the same hypothesis we may explain the somewhat paradoxical statement that Hathor is "mother of her father, daughter of her son" – that she is mother, wife, and daughter to Ra. The moon, when she appears in the heavens before the sun, may be regarded as his mother; when she reigns together with the sun she is his wife; when she rises after he has set she is

his daughter. It was as the ideal of womanhood, therefore – mother, wife, and daughter – that Hathor received the homage of Egyptian women, and became the patron deity of love, joy, and merry-making; "lady of music and mistress of song; lady of leaping, and mistress of wreathing garlands". Temples were raised in her honour, notably one of exceptional beauty at Denderah, in Upper Egypt, and she had many shrines. She became in time associated with many local goddesses, and it has been said that all Egyptian goddesses were forms of Hathor.

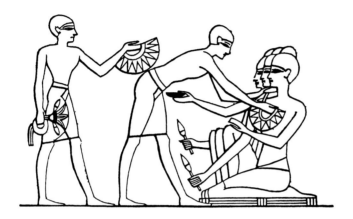

Garlands of flowers were an important aspect of Egyptian hospitality, as in this image of servants adorning house-guests.

As guardian of the dead, Hathor is shown as a cow arising from the Mountain of the West, and she is also represented as standing on its summit receiving the setting sun and the souls of the dead (the latter travelling in the footsteps of the sun-god). In this case Hathor might be regarded as the western sky, but the myth might be equally significant of the moon, which sometimes "stands on the mountains of the west" after sunset, with horns resembling hands outstretched to welcome the unseen souls.

When she was born as the daughter of Ra (her mother was Nut, the sky-goddess) Hathor was quite black. This may indicate an Ethiopian origin, or it may be that she represents the night sky, which lightens with the growth of day. It is still possible, however, to regard her as typifying the moon, which is born black, with only a narrow crescent of light, but which grows brighter as it becomes older.

The Forms of Hathor

Hathor is sometimes identified with the star Sept, or Sothis (Sirius), which rose heliacally on the first day of the month of Thoth. When Ra entered his boat Sothis, or the goddess Hathor, took her place on his head like a crown. She was identified with Aphrodite by the Greeks, and by the Egyptians with a multitude of local deities. The Seven Hathors, sometimes stated to be independent deities, were in reality but a selection of forms of the goddess, the selection varying according to locality. The Seven Hathors worshipped at Denderah were Hathor of Thebes, Hathor of Heliopolis, Hathor of Aphroditopolis, Hathor of the Sinaitic Peninsula, Hathor of Momemphis, Hathor of Herakleopolis, and Hathor of Keset. These were represented as young women carrying tambourines and wearing the Hathor headdress of a disk and a pair of horns. In the Litanies of Seker other groups of Seven Hathors are mentioned.

The sacred barque of Amen carried before Ramesses II and Queen Nefertari: a modern impression of a relief in the inner hall of the Great Temple at Abu Simbel, counterpart to the temple of Hathor.

CHAPTER III

MYTHS OF THE OSIRIS CYCLE

THE MYTH OF OSIRIS

Nut, the sky-goddess, was the wife of Ra. She was, however, beloved by Geb, whose affection she returned. When Ra discovered his wife's infidelity he was wrathful indeed, and pronounced a curse upon her, saying that the children she had conceived with Geb would not be born in any known month or year.

Now the curse of Ra the mighty could not be turned aside, for Ra was the chief of all the gods. In her distress Nut called upon the god Thoth, who also loved her. Thoth knew that the curse of Ra must be fulfilled, yet by a very cunning stratagem he found a way out of the difficulty.

He went to the moon-goddess, whose light rivalled that of the sun himself, and challenged her to a game of backgammon. The stakes on both sides were high, but the goddess staked some of her light, the seventieth part of each of her illuminations, and lost. Thus it came about that her light wanes and dwindles at certain periods, so that the moon is no longer the rival of the sun.

From the light that he had won from the moon goddess, Thoth made five days which he added to the year (at that time consisting of three hundred and sixty days) in such wise that they belonged neither to the preceding nor to the following year, nor to any month. On these five days Nut was delivered of her five children. Osiris was born on the first day, Horus on the second, Set on the third, Isis on the fourth, and Nephthys on the fifth. On the birth of Osiris a loud voice rang throughout all the world saying, "The lord of all the earth is born!"

In the course of time this prophecy concerning Osiris was fulfilled, and he became a great and wise king. The land of Egypt flourished under his rule as it had never done before. He set himself the task of civilizing his people, who until his coming had lived very barbarously, indulging in cannibalism and other such practices. He gave them a code of laws, taught them the arts of husbandry, and showed them the proper rites for worshipping the gods. And when he had succeeded in establishing law and order in Egypt set off

Osiris, the great and wise mythological king of Egypt, embraced by Isis and Nephthys and surrounded by images of other deities, from a bas-relief at Philae.

A dramatic image of sunset over the pyramids at Gizeh (opposite). The sun god Ra was the cuckolded husband of Nut, the sky goddess and mother of Osiris, Horus the Elder, Set, Isis and Nephthys.

for distant lands to continue there his work of civilization. So gentle and good was he, and such a patient teacher, that the people of those countries worshipped the very ground on which he trod.

Set, the Enemy

He had one bitter enemy, however, in his brother Set. During the absence of Osiris his wife Isis ruled the country so well that the schemes of the wicked Set to take a share in its government were not allowed to mature. But on the king's return Set fixed on a plan by which he might rid himself altogether of the king, his brother. For the accomplishment of his ends he allied himself with Aso, the queen of Ethiopia, and seventy-two other conspirators. Then, after secretly measuring the king's body, he had made a marvellous sarcophagus, richly fashioned and adorned, which would contain exactly the body of Osiris. This done, he invited his fellow-plotters and his brother the king to a great feast.

Now Osiris had frequently been warned by the queen to beware of Set, but, having no evil in himself, he did not fear it in others, so he went to the banquet. When the feast was over Set had the beautiful sarcophagus brought into the banqueting-hall, and said, as though in jest, that it should belong to him whom it would fit. One after another the guests lay down in the sarcophagus, but it fitted none of them till the turn of Osiris came. Quite unsuspicious of treachery, the king laid himself down in the great receptacle. In a moment the conspirators had nailed down the lid, pouring boiling lead over it to seal every aperture. Then they set the coffin adrift on the Nile, at its Tanaitic mouth. These things befell, say some, in the twenty-eighth year of Osiris' life; others say in the twenty-eighth year of his reign.

When the news reached the ears of Isis she was griefstricken, and cut off a lock of her hair and put on mourning clothes. Knowing well that the

The beautiful sarcophagus presented to Osiris by Set emphasizes the care devoted to the construction and decoration of sarcophagi in ancient Egypt, illustrated here by the decorated sarcophagus of Amenophis II, from the Valley of Kings.

dead cannot rest until their bodies have been buried with funeral rites, she set out to find the corpse of her husband. For a long time her search went unrewarded, though she asked every man and woman she met whether they had seen the richly decorated sarcophagus. At last it occurred to her to inquire of some children who played by the Nile and, by coincidence, they were able to tell her that the sarcophagus had been brought to the Tanaitic mouth of the Nile by Set and his accomplices. From that time onwards children were regarded by the Egyptians as having some special faculty of divination.

The Tamarisk-tree

By consulting demons, the queen learned that the sarcophagus had been cast up on the shore of Byblos, and flung by the waves into a tamarisk-bush, which had shot up miraculously into a magnificent tree, enclosing the coffin of Osiris in its trunk.

The king of that country, Melcanthus by name, was astonished at the height and beauty of the tree, and had it cut down and a pillar made from its trunk to support the roof of his palace. Within this pillar, therefore, was hidden the coffin containing the body of Osiris.

Isis hastened with all speed to Byblos, where she seated herself by the side of a fountain. She spoke not a word to anybody, until the queen's maidens approached, and these she addressed very graciously, braiding

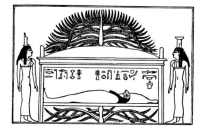

The sarcophagus of Osiris at the foot of a tamarisk bush (in some versions it is an erica tree), flanked by Isis and Nephthys, from a bas-relief at Denderah.

Female musicians and handmaidens from a wall painting in the tomb of Nakht at Luxor; the gracious behaviour of Isis to such servants of Queen Astarte led to her welcome into the queen's household.

their hair and perfuming them with her breath, more fragrant than the odour of flowers. When the maidens returned to the palace the queen inquired how it came that their hair and clothes were so delightfully perfumed, and they related their encounter with the beautiful stranger. Queen Astarte commanded that the stranger should be conducted to the palace, welcomed her graciously, and appointed her nurse to one of the young princes.

The Grief of Isis

Isis fed the boy by giving him her finger to suck. Every night, when all had retired to rest, she would pile great logs on the fire and thrust the child among them, and, changing herself into a swallow, would twitter mournful lamentations for her dead husband.

Rumours of these strange practices were brought by the queen's maidens to the ears of their mistress, who determined to see for herself whether or not there was any truth in them. So she concealed herself in the great hall, and when night came sure enough Isis barred the doors and piled logs on the fire, thrusting the child among the glowing wood.

The queen rushed forward with a loud cry and rescued her son from the flames. The goddess reproved her sternly, declaring that by her action she had deprived the young prince of immortality. Then Isis revealed her identify to the awe-stricken Astarte and told her story, begging that the pillar which supported the roof might be given to her. When her request had been granted she cut open the tree, took out the coffin containing the body of Osiris, and mourned so loudly over it that one of the young princes died of terror. Then she took the chest by sea to Egypt, being accompanied on the journey by the elder son of King Melcanthus. The tree which had held the body of the god was long preserved and worshipped at Byblos.

Arriving in Egypt, Isis opened the chest and wept long and sorely over the remains of her royal husband. But now she thought of her son Horus, whom she had left in Buto, and leaving the coffin in a secret place, she set off to search for him. Meanwhile Set, while hunting by the light of the moon, discovered the richly adorned coffin and in his rage tore the body into fourteen pieces, which he scattered throughout the country.

Learning of this fresh outrage on the body of the god, Isis took a boat of papyrus-reeds and journeyed forth once more in search of her husband's remains. After this crocodiles would not touch a papyrus boat, in case it contained the goddess, still pursuing her weary search. Whenever Isis found a portion of the corpse she buried it and built a shrine to mark the spot. It is for this reason that there are so many tombs of Osiris in Egypt.

The Vengeance of Horus

By this time Horus had reached manhood, and Osiris, returning from the Duat, where he reigned as king of the dead, encouraged him to avenge the wrongs done to his parents. Horus thereupon did battle with Set, the victory falling now to one, now to the other. At one time Set was taken captive by his enemy and given into the custody of Isis, but the latter, to her son's amazement and indignation, set him at liberty. So angry was Horus that he tore the crown from his mother's head. Thoth, however, gave her a

The mummified body of Osiris carried on the back of the crocodile-god Sobek. Isis stands to the left, while an image of the resurrected Osiris sits with his son Horus the Child (Harpocrates) in the disk of the sun.

helmet in the shape of a cow's head. (Another version states that Horus cut off his mother's head, which Thoth, the maker of magic, stuck on again in the form of a cow's.) Horus and Set, it is said, still do battle with one another, yet victory has fallen to neither. When Horus finally vanquishes his enemy, Osiris will return to earth and reign once more as king in Egypt.

Boats of papyrus reeds, built using ancient techniques, from the modern day Pharaonic Village in Cairo. Isis took such a boat in her renewed search for the remains of Osiris.

THE BLACK HOG

One day Horus sought Ra with a request to be allowed to read the future in his eyes. This request Ra granted willingly because of his love for Horus, the beloved of gods and men. While they conversed, they were watched by a black hog, a huge, sinister animal, ferocious of aspect, and with eyes that glinted with cunning and cruelty. Though neither Ra nor Horus was aware of the fact, the black hog was Set himself, who had the power to take upon him the shape of any animal he chose. "What an evil monster!" cried Ra, as he looked upon the animal.

Horus also turned his gaze in the direction of the black hog, in whom he still failed to recognize his enemy. This was Set's opportunity. He shot a bolt of fire straight into the eye of the god.

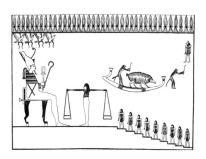

The image of the evil Set as a black hog is a common one: here Osiris sits in judgement while Set as a hog passes in a boat.

81

Horus was half crazed with the violence of the pain. "Set hath done me this evil," he cried; "he shall not go unpunished." But Set had vanished, and was not to be found anywhere. Yet for the evil that had come upon Horus, Ra cursed the pig.

When the young god recovered his sight Ra gave to him the city of Pé, at which he was much delighted; and at his smile the cloud of darkness passed away, and all the land rejoiced.

THE MYTH OF THE WINGED DISK

In the year 363 of the reign of Ra-Horakhti upon the earth it happened that the god was in Nubia with a mighty army. Set, the Evil One, had rebelled against him, for Ra was advanced in years, and Set was of all beings the most cunning and treacherous. He had slain his twin-brother Osiris, the great and good king; and for this reason Horus the Elder, the brother of Osiris, was his implacable enemy. With his chariots and horsemen and foot-soldiers, Ra embarked along the Great River and came to Edfu, where Horus joined him. "O Ra," said Horus, "great are thine enemies, and cunningly do they conspire against thee!" "My son," answered Ra, "arm thee and go forth against mine enemies, and slay them speedily." Thereupon Horus sought the aid of the god Thoth, the master of all magic, by whose aid he changed himself into a great sun-disk, with resplendent wings outstretched on either side. Straight to the sun he flew, and from the heavens he looked so fiercely upon his enemies that their perceptions became confused. Each man judged his neighbour to be a stranger, and a cry went up that the foe were upon them. Each turned his weapons against the other, the majority were slain, and the handful of survivors scattered. And Horus hovered for a while over the battle-plain, hoping to find Set, but the arch-enemy was not there; he was hiding in the North Country.

Then Horus returned to Ra, who embraced him kindly. And Horus took Ra and the goddess Hathor, and showed them the battlefield strewn with corpses. Ra, king of the gods, said to those in his train: "Come, let us voyage to the Nile, for our enemies are slain." But Set still had a large following, and he commanded some of his associates to turn themselves into crocodiles and hippopotami, so that they might attack the occupants of the divine barque while remaining invulnerable because of their thick

The great winged sun-disk, into which the god of wisdom changed Horus the Elder to facilitate his revenge on the fratricidal Set.

An early image of a hippopotamus warrior-goddess. Both the hippopotamus and the crocodile were regarded with fear and a certain magical reverence by the Egyptians, making them appropriate accomplices of Set.

Crocodiles shown in a wall relief at the temple of Sobek, the crocodile god, at Kom Ombo.

A lion in a relief carving at Luxor.
Horus' adoption of the form of a lion
in his last battles against Set reflects
the symbolic importance of the lion in
the Nubian desert, where they were
common until Roman times.

hides. Horus, however, had gathered a band of smiths, each of whom made for himself an iron lance and a chain, on which Thoth bestowed some of his ever-powerful magic. Horus also repeated the formulae in the *Book of Slaying the Hippopotamus*. When the fierce animals charged up the river the god was ready for them; many of them were pierced by the magic weapons and died, while the remainder fled.

Those who fled to the south were pursued by Horus, and were at length overtaken. Another great conflict ensued, in which the followers of Set were again vanquished. On the orders of Ra, a shrine was raised on the battlefield to commemorate the victor, and his image placed in it. Yet another encounter, however, was to take place, in the South Land, before the followers of Set were utterly destroyed.

The Slaughter of the Monsters

Then Horus and Ra sailed northward toward the sea in search of Set and his allies, intending to slay all the crocodiles and hippopotami. But the beasts kept under water, and four days had elapsed before Horus caught sight of them. He attacked them at once, and wrought great havoc with his glittering weapons, to the delight of Ra and Thoth, who watched the conflict from the boat. A hundred and forty-two prisoners were taken on this occasion. But Horus continued to pursue his enemies, always in the form of a burning disk with wings like the sunset, and attended by the goddesses Nekhbet and Uazet in the shape of two snakes.

Once more he overtook the allies of Set, this time at the Western Waters of Mert. On this occasion, as on the others, Horus was victorious, and nearly four hundred prisoners were brought to the boat of Ra and slain.

Set was very greatly incensed, and decided to come forth in person to do battle with Horus. Horrible indeed were his cries and curses when he heard the losses his army had sustained. Horus and his followers went out to meet the army of Set, and the battle was long and furious.

At last Horus took a prisoner whom he believed to be Set. The wretched being was dragged before Ra, who gave him into the hands of his captor, bidding the latter do with him what he would. Horus killed his prisoner by cutting off his head, dragged him through the dust, and cut his body in pieces, just as Set had done to Osiris. Unfortunately, however, the prisoner was only one of Set's associates. The Evil One himself was still at large, vowing vengeance on his enemies. Disguised as a large snake, he hid himself under the earth, while his followers took courage from the knowledge that he had eluded his enemy. Yet again, however, they were defeated by Horus, who slew great numbers of them.

The gods remained for six days on the canal, waiting for the reappearance of the foe, but none were to be seen. Then Horus scattered abroad his followers to destroy the remnant of Set's army.

The last two battles were fought at Thalu, and at Shais, in Nubia. At Thalu Horus took the form of a fierce lion, and slew a hundred-and-forty-two enemies. At Shais he appeared once more in the shape of a great shining disk with wings of splendid plumage, and with the goddesses Nekhbet and Uazet on either side of it in the shape of crowned snakes. On these occasions also Horus was victorious.

There are various endings to this myth. In one version the prisoner whom Horus decapitated was indeed Set, but he was reincarnated in the form of a serpent. According to this version Horus of Edfu was accompanied by Horus the Child, son of Isis and Osiris (the two Horuses are utterly confused in the account of the battles: while Horus the Elder fights the battles, Horus the Child kills Set). According to one account, Horus delivered the captive Set into the hands of Isis, who cut off his bead. Another version (page 80) has it that the decisive battle has not yet been fought, and that Horus will finally destroy his enemy, when Osiris and the gods once more return to earth.

Other Horus Legends

Another legend states that when Horus the Child had become a man Set came forth and challenged him to mortal combat. So Horus set out in a boat splendidly decorated by Isis, who also laid magic spells upon it, so that its occupant might not be overcome. Meanwhile the arch-foe of the gods had taken upon himself the shape of a huge red hippopotamus. He caused a raging storm to break over the boats of Horus and his train, so that the waters were lashed into fury; and had it not been that the boats were protected by magic, all would certainly have perished. Horus, however, held to his course undismayed. He had taken the form of a youth of giant stature, and towered over the gilded prow of his boat, which shone like sunlight amid the storm and the darkness. A great harpoon was poised in his hand, larger than an ordinary mortal could lift. In the water the red hippopotamus waited for the wrecking of the boat, so that he might attack his enemies. But as soon as he showed himself above water the mighty harpoon was launched at his head and sank into his brain. And this was the end of Set, the Evil One, the murderer of Osiris and the enemy of Ra. In honour of Horus the Conqueror hymns and triumphal choruses were sung throughout the land.

Horus the Younger harpooning Set in the form of a red hippopotamus, with the assistance of Isis.

CHAPTER IV

MYTHS OF THE GREAT GODS

THE SLAYING OF MEN

The following story reveals the goddess Hathor in her most fearsome aspect, as the Eye of Ra – in this case almost certainly the moon, felt by the Egyptians to be capable of holding back the annual Nile flood. The vengeance of Ra is doubtless the plagues and starvation that accompany the dry season immediately before the flood; the beer represents the flood itself. The Festival of the Intoxication of Hathor was held in the month of Thoth, the first month of the flood.

Long ago there dwelt on earth Ra, the sun-god, the creator of men and things, and ruler over the gods. For a time men gave to him the reverence due to his exalted position, but at length he began to grow old, and they mocked him, saying; "Behold! his bones are like silver, his limbs are like gold, his hair is like unto real lapis-lazuli." Ra became angry when he heard their blasphemy, so he called together his followers, the gods and goddesses of his train, Shu and Tefnut, Geb and Nut, and Hathor, the Eye of Ra.

The gods assembled secretly, so that the race of mankind might know nothing of their meeting. And when they were all gathered about the throne of Ra, he said to Nun, the oldest of the gods: "O Nun, thou first-born of the gods, whose son I am, I pray thee give me thy counsel. The men whom I have created have conceived evil against me, even those men who have issued forth from mine eye. They have murmured in their hearts, saying, 'Behold! the king has become old, his bones are like silver, his limbs like gold, his hair like unto real lapis-lazuli.' Tell me, what shall be done unto them? For this have I sought thy counsel. I will not destroy them till thou hast spoken."

Then Nun answered: "O thou great god, who art greater than he who made thee, thou son who art mightier than his father, do thou but turn thine eye upon them who blaspheme thee, and they shall perish from off the earth."

Ra turned his eye upon the blasphemers, as Nun had advised. But the men fled and hid in deserts and rocky places. Then all the gods and goddesses gave counsel to Ra that he should send his eye down among men

A wall painting of Hathor, goddess of love, in her human and most benificent form, from the tomb of Horemheb in the Valley of Kings. In "The Slaying of Men" she takes the more destructive manifestation of the Eye of Ra.

The Nile in flood (opposite). The story of "The Slaying of Men" emphasizes the disastrous consequences for the Egyptian population of a failure of the Nile flood.

Hathor's intoxication reflected Egyptian attitudes to alcohol: the excessive consumption of wine or beer was not uncommon among the nobility, in women as well as men, as this caricature reveals.

to attack them. The Eye of Ra descended in the form of the goddess Hathor, and struck the men in the desert, killing them. Then Hathor returned to the court of Ra, and when the king had given her welcome she said, "I have been mighty among mankind. It is well pleasing to my heart."

All night Sekhmet waded in the blood of those who had been slain, and Ra feared that on the next day Hathor would kill the remnant of the human race, so he said unto his attendants, "Fetch to me swift messengers who can outstrip the wind." When the messengers appeared, Ra bade them bring a great number of mandrakes from Elephantine. These Ra gave to Sekhmet, bidding her to pound them, and when this was done he mixed the mandrakes with some of the blood of those whom Hathor had slain. Meanwhile servant-maids were busy preparing beer from barley, and into this Ra poured the mixture. Seven thousand jars of beer were made.

In the morning Ra ordered his attendants to carry the beer to the place where Hathor would seek to slay the remnant of mankind, and there pour it out. The sun-god had said to himself, "I will deliver mankind out of her hands."

At dawn Hathor reached the place where the beer lay, flooding the fields four spans deep. She was pleased with her beautiful reflection, which smiled at her from the floods; and drank so deeply of the beer that she became intoxicated, and was no longer able to destroy the humans.

Thereafter, festivals were celebrated with great revelry in commemoration of this event.

Egyptian festivals frequently involved great revelry, as indicated in these images of guests being carried home from a drinking party.

THE PRINCESS AND THE DEMON

Central to the following story is the Egyptian belief that a temple statue contained a real incarnation of the god it represented. The god Khonsu features here in two of his aspects, co-operating against a demon or ghost possessing the daughter of a Syrian vassal of the Pharoah.

In the reign of Pharoah Ramesses there were many fair women in Egypt, but lovelier than them all was the daughter of the prince of Bekhten, one of the king's vassals. She was tall and slender and very shapely, of exquisite form and feature, and there was nothing on earth with which to compare her beauty, so men compared it with the beauty of Amen-Ra, the light of day.

Now Ramesses was a great conqueror and a mighty man of valour, who numbered among his vassals princes of no mean degree. These latter came every year to Nahairana, at the mouth of the Euphrates, to do homage to their overlord and to render tribute to him. Rich indeed was the tribute that the king received, for every prince who bowed before him was accompanied by a retinue of slaves bearing gold and precious stones and sweet-smelling woods, the choicest things that their various dominions could afford.

Egyptian princesses were able to devote a good deal of time and energy to their appearance. This modern impression of a painting from the tomb of Queen Nefertari shows a typically elaborate headdress and makeup.

On one such occasion Ramesses and his princes were gathered at Nahairana, and the vassals vied with each other in the splendour of their offerings. But the Prince of Bekhten had a treasure which far surpassed that of the others, for he had brought his beautiful daughter. When Pharoah saw her he loved her beyond all else, and wished to make her his wife. For the rest of the tribute he cared nothing, and the homage of the remaining princes bored him. So he married the princess, and gave to her a name which signifies "Beauty of Ra". And the queen was beloved of her husband and her people.

Some idea of the dignity of Egyptian princes can be gained from this wall painting from a prince's tomb in the Valley of Queens.

Now it came about that on the festival of the god Amen, when the sacred barque is born aloft for all to see, the king and queen went up to the temple to do honour to the sun-god. And while they worshipped, attendants sought them with the news that a messenger from the Prince of Bekhten waited outside and wished to speak to them. The king bade that the messenger be admitted. He brought rich gifts from the Prince of Bekhten to his daughter, the Great Royal Wife, while to the king he bowed very low, saying: "Behold, O king, the little sister of the Great Royal Wife lies ill. I pray thee, therefore, to send a physician to heal her of her malady." Then the king called his wise men about him and deliberated whom he should send to the succour of his wife's sister. At length the wise men brought before the king one of their number, a scribe named Tehuti-em-heb, who was accordingly appointed to accompany the messenger to Bekhten, there to heal the queen's sister, Bent-reshy.

But when they reached the domain of the Prince of Bekhten, Tehuti-em-heb found that the demon who was the cause of the princess's affliction was far too powerful to be expelled by his skill. When the maid's father heard that the Egyptian scribe was powerless to cast out the demon he fell into despair, thinking his last hope had gone. But Tehuti-em-heb comforted him as best he might, bidding him send once more to Egypt to beseech the intervention of the god Khonsu, Expeller of Demons, on his daughter's behalf. So the Lord of Bekhten sent yet another messenger to the court of Ramesses.

Now the land of Bekhten was far from the land of Egypt, and the journey between them occupied a year and five months. When the messenger of the Prince of Bekhten reached Egypt he found Ramesses in Thebes, in the temple of Khonsu, for it was the month which was sacred to that god. The messenger bowed before Ramesses and gave him the message sent by the queen's father.

In the temple at Thebes there were two statues of the god Khonsu, one called Khonsu in Thebes Neferhetep, the other Khonsu, Expeller of Demons, both representing the god as a handsome youth. Ramesses approached Khonsu in Thebes Neferhetep and prayed that he would permit Khonsu, the Expeller of Demons, to go to the land of Bekhten for the healing of Bent-reshy, the queen's little sister. Khonsu in Thebes Neferhetep bowed his assent, and gave his protection to the Expeller of Demons. When this was done Khonsu, Expeller of Demons, was dispatched to Bekhten, accompanied by a large retinue, and with ceremony befitting a king. They journeyed for a year and five months, and at length reached the land of the queen's father. The prince himself and all his people hastened to greet Khonsu, prostrating themselves and offering rich gifts even as they might have done to the King of Egypt himself. Meanwhile Bent-reshy's illness had continued unabated, for the demon who possessed her was very potent. But when Khonsu was conducted to her chamber, behold! she grew well in a moment, to the joy of her father and his courtiers. The demon who had come out of her acknowledged Khonsu as his superior, and those who stood by heard with awe a conversation pass between them.

"O Khonsu," said the spirit, "I am thy slave. If thou commandest that I go from hence, I will go. But I pray thee ask of the Prince of Bekhten that he will make a holy day for me and a sacrifice. Then shall I go in peace."

"It shall be as thou hast said," replied Khonsu, and he commanded the Prince of Bekhten to make a sacrifice and a holy day for the demon who had possessed Bent-reshy.

First the people made a great sacrifice to Khonsu, the Expeller of Demons; then they made one for the demon, who thereafter departed in peace. But when he had gone the mind of the Prince of Bekhten was grievously troubled, for he thought: "Perchance he will come again unto our land, and torment the people even as he has tormented my daughter, Bent-reshy." So he determined that Khonsu, the Expeller of Demons, must not be allowed to depart from Bekhten, but must be kept there always, lest the demon should return.

For more than three years, therefore, the Prince of Bekhten kept Khonsu within his domains, and would not allow him to depart. But one night he had a dream which altered his determination. In his dream he

Camels before the pyamids. The messenger of the Prince of Bekhten would have made his journey to Egypt using the long-distance caravan routes whose origins stretch back to prehistory.

stood before the shrine of Khonsu, Expeller of Demons. And as he looked, behold! the doors of the shrine were flung wide, and the god himself issued forth, took the form of a hawk with wonderful golden plumage, and flew toward Egypt. When he awoke the Lord of Bekhten knew that the real god had departed to Egypt, and that it was useless to keep any longer his statue. Moreover, he feared the vengeance of Khonsu. So on the morrow he loaded the statue of Khonsu, the Expeller of Demons, with rich and beautiful gifts, and sent him away to Egypt with a princely retinue.

When the return journey was accomplished Khonsu, Expeller of Demons, bestowed all the costly gifts on Khonsu in Thebes Neferhetep, keeping nothing for himself of all he had received.

Avenue of rams at Karnak. The god Khnemu, a god particularly associated with Elephantine Island and the Nile cataracts, was frequently depicted with a ram's head.

THE LEGEND OF THE NILE'S SOURCE

The following story deals with the powers ascribed to the god Khnemu over the most important event in the Egyptian calendar, the annual flood of the Nile. The inscription from which it is taken was carved on a rock on the island of Sahal in the Nile during the Ptolemaic period.

In the eighteenth year of the reign of Djoser, the third monarch of the Third Dynasty, a famine spread over Egypt because for seven years the Nile had not risen in flood. Thus grain of all kinds was scarce, the fields and gardens yielded naught, so that the people had no food. Strong men tottered like the aged, the old fell to the ground and rose no more, the children cried aloud with the pangs of hunger. And for the little food there was men became thieves and robbed their neighbours.

Reports of these terrible conditions reached the king upon his throne, and he was stricken with grief. He remembered the god Imhotep, the son of Ptah, who had once delivered Egypt from a like disaster, but when his help was invoked no answer was forthcoming.

Then Djoser the king sent to his governor Mater who ruled over the South, the island of Elephantine and Nubia, and asked him where was the source of the Nile and what was the name of the god or goddess of the river. And to answer this dispatch Mater the governor went in person before the king. He told him of the wonderful island of Elephantine, whereon was built the first city ever known; that out of it rose the sun when he wanted to bestow life upon mankind. Here also was a double cavern, Querti, in shape like two breasts, and from this cavern rose the Nile flood to bless the land with fruitfulness when the god drew back the bolts of the door at the proper season. And this god was Khnemu.

Mater described to his royal master the temple of the Nile at Elephantine, and stated that other gods were in it, including the great deities Osiris, Horus, Isis and Nephthys. He told of the products of the country around, and said that from these, offerings should be made to Khnemu.

Then the king rose and offered sacrifices unto the god and made supplication before him in his temple. And the god heard and appeared before the grief-stricken king. He said, "I am Khnemu the Creator. My hands rest upon thee to protect thy person and to make sound thy body. I gave thee thine heart... I am he who created himself. I am the primeval watery abyss, and I am the Nile who riseth at his will to give health to those who toil. I am the guide and director of all men, the Almighty, the father of the gods, Shu, the mighty possessor of the earth." And then the god promised the king that henceforward the Nile should rise every year as in the past, that the famine should be ended and great good come upon the land.

But also he told the king how his shrine was desolate and that no one troubled to restore it even although stone lay all around. And this the king remembered and made a royal decree that lands on each side of the Nile near the island where Khnemu dwelt were to be set apart as the endowment of his temple, that priests were to minister at his shrine, and for their maintenance a tax must be levied on the products of the land near by. And this decree the king caused to be cut upon a stone stele and set up in a prominent place as a lasting token of gratitude unto the god Khnemu, the god of the Nile.

A temple complex on Elephantine, one of the largest islands in the Nile. Situated near Aswan and the First Cataract, it was an important centre near Egypt's southern border from the time of the Old Kingdom.

CHAPTER V

TALES FROM EGYPTIAN HISTORY

THE DREAM OF THOTHMES

The following story, relating a dream of the Pharaoh Thothmes IV, was found on a stele contained in a small temple between the paws of the great Sphinx near the pyramid at Gizeh. The end of the inscription was so defaced as to be indecipherable.

There was a king in Egypt called Thothmes, a mighty monarch, skilled in the arts of war and of the chase. He was fair to look upon, too, with a beauty like that of Horus, whom Isis bore in the Northern Marshes, and greatly was he loved by gods and men.

He enjoyed hunting in the burning desert, alone or with only a few companions, and this is told of one of his hunting expeditions.

One day, before he had ascended the throne of Egypt, he was hunting unattended in the desert. It was noon, and the sun beat fiercely down upon him so that he wished to seek the shadow of the mighty Harmachis, the Sphinx. Great and powerful was the god, and very majestic was his image, with the face of a man and the body of a lion, a snake upon his brow. In many temples were sacrifices made to him; in many towns did men worship with their faces turned toward him. In the great cool shadow Thothmes laid himself down to rest, and sleep enchained his senses. And as he slept he dreamed, and behold! the Sphinx opened its lips and spoke to him; it was no longer a thing of motionless rock, but the god himself, the great Harmachis. And he addressed the dreamer thus:

"Behold me, O Thothmes, for I am the Sun-god, the ruler of all peoples. Harmachis is my name, and Ra, and Khepra, and Tem. I am thy father, and thou art my son, and through me shall all good come upon thee if thou wilt hearken to my words. The land of Egypt shall be thine, and the North Land, and the South Land. In prosperity and happiness shalt thou rule for many years." He paused, and it seemed to Thothmes as if the god were struggling to free himself from the overwhelming sands, for only his head was visible.

"It is as thou seest," Harmachis resumed; "the sands of the desert are over me. Do that quickly which I command thee, O my son Thothmes."

Before Thothmes could reply the vision faded and he awoke. The living god was gone, and in his place was the mighty image of the Sphinx, hewn from the solid rock.

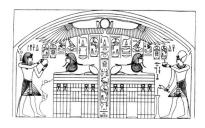

A drawing taken from the dream stele, showing Thothmes making offerings to the Sphinx.

The dominating form of the Sphinx (opposite), with the stele between its paws on which the story of "The Dream of Thothmes" was inscribed.

CIVIL WAR IN EGYPT

This story is one of two surviving tales from the so-called Petoubastis cycle, apparently relating to historical events during the reign of the pharaoh of that name during the Twenty-third Dynasty. The second story, "The Theft of the Throne", is almost identical, but takes place some years later in the reign of Petoubastis. The two stories survived in papyri dating from the second and first centuries AD respectively.

The Theft of the Cuirass

In the reign of the Pharaoh Petoubastis the Delta and a great part of Lower Egypt were divided into two rival factions, one part being headed by Kamenophis, Prince of Mendes, and the other ruled by the king-priest of Heliopolis, Ierharerou, and his ally Pakrourou, the great lord of the east. Only four nomes in the middle of the Delta were subject to Kamenophis, whilst Ierharerou had succeeded in establishing his children or relations in power in most of the other nomes.

Ierharerou possessed a cuirass to which he attached great value and which was generally regarded as a talisman. At his death Kamenophis, taking advantage of the mourning and confusion in Heliopolis, seized the cuirass and placed it in one of his own strongholds. Prince Pimonî "the Little" – "Pimonî of the strong fist", as he is sometimes called in the narrative – the successor of Ierharerou, demanded its restoration. Kamenophis refused, and hence arose a quarrel in which all the provinces of Egypt were implicated.

A noble warrior, about to loose an arrow from a lightly constructed two-horse chariot, taken from a modern copy of an Egyptian painting.

Pimonî and Pakrourou both presented themselves before King Petoubastis, asking his permission to be revenged on Kamenophis; but Pharaoh, who knew that this would entail civil war, endeavoured to dissuade Pimonî from taking steps against Kamenophis and, indeed, forbade him to proceed with his intentions, promising as compensation a splendid funeral for Ierharerou. Unwillingly Pimonî submitted, but after the funeral ceremonies were over resentment still burned within him, and he and Pakrourou, "the great ruler of the east", returned again to Petoubastis at his court in Tanis. He received them rather impatiently, asking them why they troubled him again and declaring that he would not allow civil war during his reign. They, however, would not be satisfied and said they could not go on with the celebration of the feast that was to follow the religious rites of Ierharerou's funeral until the shield or cuirass was restored to its rightful owner.

Pharaoh then sent for Kamenophis, and requested him urgently to return the shield, but in vain. Kamenophis declined to do so.

Then said Pimonî, "By Tem, the lord of Heliopolis, the great god, my god, were it not for Pharaoh's decree and that my respect for him protects you, I should kill you this very instant."

Kamenophis replied, "By the life of Mendes, the great god, the war which will break out in the nome, the battle which will break out in the city will stir up clan against clan, and man against man, before the cuirass shall be wrested from the stronghold where I have placed it."

The Horrors of War

Pakrourou then said before the king, "Is it right what Kamenophis has done, and are not the words he has just spoken said to provoke us to anger, that we may measure our strength against his? I will make Kamenophis and the nome of Mendes feel the shame of these words uttered to provoke the civil war which Pharaoh has forbidden; I will glut them with war. I said nothing because I knew the king did not want war; but if the king remains neutral I shall be silent no longer, and the king shall see all the horrors of civil war."

Pharaoh said, "Be neither boastful nor timid, Pakrourou, great ruler of the east, but now go each one of you to your nomes and your towns in peace, and give me but five days, and I swear by Amen-Ra that I shall cause the cuirass to be put back in the place from which it was taken." Pimonî then said that if the cuirass were replaced nothing more should be said about it, and there should be no war; but if it were withheld, he would fight for it, against the whole of Egypt if necessary.

Kamenophis at this respectfully asked and obtained permission from Pharaoh to order all his men to arm themselves, and to go with him to the Lake of the Gazelle and prepare to fight.

Then Pimonî, encouraged by Pakrourou, sent messages of a similar import to his nomes and cities. Pakrourou further advised him to hasten to the Lake of the Gazelle and be there before Kamenophis had assembled all his men, and Pimonî, with only one band of men, took his advice and was first in the field, intending to wait there till his brothers, at the head of their respective clans, should join him.

A reconstruction of a bronze corselet from the tomb of Ramesses III. The typical Egyptian corselet was a coat of scale-armour, with rows of metal plates secured by pins that allowed some flexibility as well as providing protection.

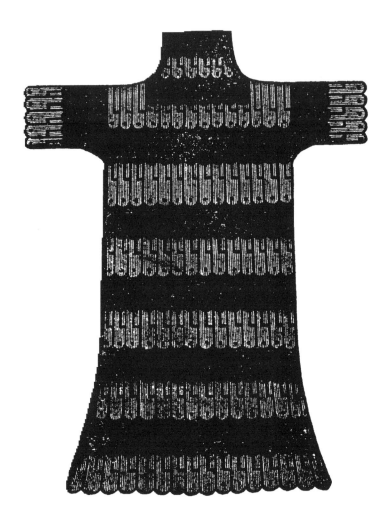

Egyptian warriors attacking from the prow of a ship or barge. Large numbers of soldiers could be transported much more quickly via the Nile than by marching over land.

News of this was taken to Kamenophis, and he hastily assembled the troops of his four nomes, Tanis, Mendes, Tahait, and Sebennytos. Arriving at the lake, he at once challenged Pimonî to single combat, and Pimonî, though his own forces had not yet arrived, accepted the challenge.

Pimonî put on a shirt of byssus (linen cloth) embroidered with silver and gold, and over that a second shirt of linen; he also donned his bronze corselet and carried two golden swords; he put on his helmet and sallied forth to meet Kamenophis.

While they were fighting, Zinonfi, Pimonî's young servant, ran off to watch for the forces that were to come to Pimonî's aid, and he soon descried a flotilla so large that the river could hardly carry all the barges. They were the people of Heliopolis coming to help their lord. As soon as they came within earshot Zinonfi called out to them to hurry, because Pimonî was being hard pressed by Kamenophis, which, indeed, was true, for his horse was slain under him.

Kamenophis redoubled his efforts when he saw the fresh forces arriving, and Petekhousou, Pimonî's brother, challenged Anoukhoron, the Pharoah's son, to single combat. When Pharaoh heard this he was very angry. He went in person to the field of battle and forbade the combatants to proceed, and also commanded a truce until all the forces should be assembled.

Petoubastis and all the chieftains occupied prominent positions so that they could watch what was going on, and the men were as numerous as the

A troop of Egyptian archers, equipped with axes and clubs as well as their bows, led by a standard-bearer.

sands of the seashore and their rage against each other uncontrollable. The troops of the four nomes were ranged behind Kamenophis, and the soldiers of the nome of Heliopolis behind Pimonî the Little.

Then Petoubastis gave Pakrourou a signal, and he armed himself and went down among the forces, stirring them all to deeds of valour; he pitted man against man, and great was the ardour he aroused in them.

Succour for Pakrourou

After Pakrourou had left the melée, he met a mighty man in armour in command of forty galleys and eight thousand soldiers. This was Moutoubaal, a prince of Syria, who had been warned in a dream to repair to the Lake of the Gazelle to help to regain the stolen cuirass. Pakrourou gave him a place, though all the forces were now disposed; but he ordered him not to join in the fight until the opposite side – the men of Kamenophis – should attack their vessels. Moutoubaal's troops therefore remained in their ships, and Pakrourou went back to his point of vantage to watch the progress of the battle.

The two factions fought from four in the morning to nine in the evening. Finally the forces of Anoukhoron, the king's son, broke under the pressure of attacks from the men of Sebennytos and they fled toward the boats. Then Moutoubaal took his opportunity and advanced against the troops of Sebennytos and routed them. He went on spreading destruction among the forces of Kamenophis, until Pharaoh came up with Pakrourou and besought him to stay his hand, promising that he would see to it that the shield was restored.

A file of well-disciplined Egyptian soldiers, each equipped with a spear, shield and hand-axe, with their section leader (left) and a trumpeter.

A modern reproduction of one of the most famous images of Egyptian warfare; the attack by Ramesses II (in the chariot) on the Hittite fortress of Dapur in Syria.

Moutoubaal accordingly halted his men after having wrought great havoc among the men of Kamenophis. Then Pharaoh and Pakrourou went with Moutoubaal to the place where Pimonî was found engaged in mortal combat with Kamenophis. Pimonî had got the upper hand and was about to slay his adversary, but they stopped him, and Pharaoh ordered Kamenophis to lay down his arms.

After this Anoukhoron, the royal prince, was overthrown by Petekhousou, the brother of Pimonî, but Pharaoh again interposed and persuaded Petekhousou to spare his son, so the young man was allowed to withdraw unhurt.

The king said, "By Amen-Ra, the sceptre has fallen from the hands of Kamenophis, prince of Mendes, Petekhousou has vanquished my son, and the bands of the four strongest nomes in Egypt have been overthrown."

The Shield Regained

An image of an Egyptian warrior, who has disarmed his opponent and is about to deliver the coup-de-grace with a long dagger. Pimonî, on the other hand, was prevented from killing Kamenophis.

Then Minnemai, Prince of the Eupuantine and the son of Ierharerou, the priest-king to whom the shield had belonged, advanced from Thebes with all his forces. They assigned him a place opposite the ship of Takhos, the chief soldier of the nome of Mendes, and it happened that in the galley of Takhos lay the cuirass itself. And Minnemai called upon his gods to let him behold his father's cuirass that he might be the instrument of its recapture. He armed himself, advanced with his men on the galley of Takhos, and confronted the nine thousand soldiers guarding the cuirass of Ierharerou, son of Osiris.

Minnemai placed thirty-four guards on the gangplank of the galley to prevent anyone from getting off, and he fell upon the soldiers guarding the cuirass. Takhos fought well and killed fifty-four men, but finally gave in and retired to his vessel, where Minnemai followed him with his Ethiopian warriors. The children of Ierharerou supported him, and they seized the cuirass of Ierharerou.

Thus was the cuirass recaptured and brought back to its former place.

There was great joy among the children of Ierharerou and the troops of Heliopolis. They went before Pharaoh and said to him, "Great master, have the history of the war of the cuirass written, and the names of the warriors who waged it, that posterity may know what a war was made in Egypt on account of the cuirass, in the nomes and in the cities; then cause the history to be engraved on a stone stele in the temple of Heliopolis." And King Petoubastis did as they asked.

A body of Egyptian troops. Their varied equipment, including curved swords, hand axes, bows and (far right) body armour, suggests soldiers of several different units are shown.

THE BIRTH OF HATSHEPSUT

Though not strictly historical, the following story recounts the birth of the historical queen Hatshepsut, who ruled Egypt from 1503 to 1482 BC in place of her son Thothmes III. It clearly reflects propaganda put out by the queen herself during her reign.

In the land of the gods Amen-Ra held court. King of the gods was Amen-Ra, and the maker of men. On his right was Osiris, with the twin goddesses Isis and Nephthys, Hathor the goddess of love, and Horus and Anubis. On his left was Mentu, the god of war, with Geb, the earth-god, and Nut, the sky-goddess, the gods Atmu and Shu, and the goddess Tefnut. And to the assembled gods Amen-Ra spoke thus:

"I will make a great queen, who shall rule over Egypt and Syria, Nubia and Punt, so that all lands may be united under her sway. Worthy must the maiden be of her great dominions, for she shall rule the whole world." As he spoke the god Thoth entered, he who has the form of an ibis, that he may fly more swiftly than the swiftest arrow. In silence he listened to the words of Amen-Ra, the mightiest of the gods, the maker of men. Then he said : "Behold, O Amen-Ra, there is in the land of Egypt a maiden of wondrous beauty. The sun in his circuit shines not on anything more fair. Surely it is fitting that she be the mother of the great queen of whom thou speakest."
"Thou sayest well," said Amen-Ra. "Where shall we seek this fair princess? What is her name?"

"Her name is Aahmes," answered Thoth. "She is wife to the King of Egypt, and dwelleth in his palace. I will lead thee to her."

"It is well," said Amen-Ra.

Then Thoth, in the shape of an ibis, flew toward the land of Egypt, and

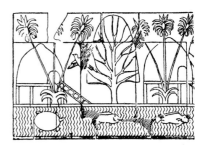

A village in the land of Punt, drawn from an Egyptian original. As well as unusual marine fauna, the drawing shows a variety of trees and houses raised on stilts.

with him went Amen-Ra, in the form of the King of Egypt, and all the gods and goddesses, among them Neith, goddess of Sais, and the scorpion goddess, Selk, on whose head was a scorpion bearing in each claw the sign of life.

Silently the gods and goddesses entered the sleeping palace, and were conducted by Thoth to the chamber of Queen Aahmes. The queen lay asleep on a couch shaped like a lion, and as they gazed upon her they saw that Thoth had spoken truly, that she was indeed the fairest of mortal women, and they stood speechless with admiration for her beauty. But the fragrance that they had borne with them from the land of Punt awoke the maiden, who looked with astonishment on her supernatural visitors. Very magnificent was Amen-Ra, the king of the gods, the maker of men, as he stood before the queen. Jewels of gold and precious stones adorned his person, and his beauty was as the beauty of the sun, so that the maiden's heart was filled with delight. Amen-Ra placed in her hand the sign of life and the emblem of power, and the goddesses Neith and Selk raised her

The dwarfish, leonine-featured Bes, a domestic god particularly regarded as helping women in childbirth, from a relief at Denderah. According to the legend, he was one of the gods present at Hatshepsut's birth.

couch above the ground, so that she might be above the earth while she conversed with the gods.

At length the gods returned to the land of Punt, and Amen-Ra called for Khnemu, the creator, the fashioner of the bodies of men.

"Fashion for me," said Amen-Ra, "the body of my daughter, and the body of her ka. A great queen shall I make of her, and honour and power shall be hers all the days of her life."

"O Amen-Ra," answered Khnemu, the creator, "it shall be done as thou hast said. The beauty of thy daughter shall surpass that of the gods, and shall be worthy of her dignity and glory."

So Khnemu fashioned the body of Amen-Ra's daughter and the body of her ka, the two forms exactly alike, and more beautiful than the daughters of men. He fashioned them of clay with the aid of his potter's wheel, and Hekt, goddess of birth, knelt by his side, holding the sign of life toward the clay that the bodies of Hatshepsut and her ka might be filled with the breath of life.

Then did the gods bring the bodies to the Palace of the King of Egypt. Khnemu, the creator, and Hekt, the goddess of birth, Isis, the great mother, and her twin sister Nephthys, Bes, the protector of children, and Meskhent and Ta-urt, all were present to hail the birth of Hatshepsut, the great queen, the daughter of Amen-Ra and Queen Aahmes.

Great were the rejoicings when the child was born, and loud the praises chanted in her honour. And in time she became ruler of all countries, rich and powerful and beloved of Amen-Ra, the great queen for whom she had been designed by the king of the gods.

In the valley of the Nile there was erected a temple to Queen Hatshepsut. The temple stands to this day, and is now known as Deir-el-Bahari, the Northern Convent.

The temple of Queen Hatshepsut at Deir el-Bahari, Western Thebes, opposite Luxor. Among the surviving reliefs is one showing the great Egyptian expedition to Punt mounted in Hatshepsut's reign, and the African goods brought back to Egypt.

A large jar of the type commonly used for storage in ancient Egypt. Thoutii's use of such jars as a means of smuggling his men into the besieged town of Joppa recalls Homer's account of the Wooden Horse at Troy.

HOW THOUTII TOOK THE TOWN OF JOPPA

This tale recounts an incident during the campaign of Thothmes III in Palestine. The beginning of the story is lost. The method employed by the wily Thoutii to smuggle his troops into the recalcitrant city recalls the tale of Ali Baba in the Thousand and One Nights.

In the reign of Thothmes III, Pharaoh of Egypt, the Prince of Joppa rose in rebellion and murdered all the Egyptian soldiers that were quartered in the town. This news naturally excited Pharaoh's wrath, and he called together his nobles and generals and scribes to see what could be done. None of them, however, had any suggestion to make except Thoutii, a brilliant young infantry officer.

"Give me," he begged, "your magic cane, O my king, and a body of infantry and of charioteers, and I undertake to kill the Prince of Joppa and to take the town."

Pharaoh, who esteemed this officer highly and knew his worth, granted all that he asked – a not immodest request, for the cane was a talisman supposed to render invisible anyone into whose possession it fell.

Thoutii then marched to Palestine with his men. Having arrived there, he had a large skin bag made, big enough to hold a man, and he had irons made for feet and hands, one pair being especially large and strong; also shackles and yokes of wood, and four hundred jars. Then he sent to the Prince of Joppa the following message:

"I am Thoutii, the Egyptian infantry general. King Thothmes was jealous of my bravery and sought to kill me; but I have escaped from him, and I have stolen his magic cane, which is hidden in my baggage; and, if you like, I will give it to you, and I will join forces with you, I and my men, the pick of the Egyptian army."

This message was very pleasant news to the Prince of Joppa, for he knew Thoutii's reputation, and knew that he had no equal in all Egypt. He sent a message to Thoutii, accepting his offer, and promising him a share of his territory. He then left Joppa, taking with him his equerry and the women and children, to greet the man whom he took to be a new and powerful ally. He welcomed him warmly, and invited him into his camp to dine with him. In course of conversation, as they were eating and drinking together, he asked Thoutii about the magic cane. Thoutii replied that it was concealed in the baggage with which his horses were laden, and requested that his men and horses should be brought into the camp to be refreshed and rested.

This was done: his horses were fed and tied up, the baggage was searched, and the magic cane found.

The Stratagem

Hearing this, the Prince of Joppa expressed his eager wish to behold the magic cane. Thoutii went and fetched it; then suddenly seizing the Prince by his clothes, he said, "Behold here King Thothmes' magic cane." And with that he raised his hand and struck the Prince on the forehead so that the latter fell down unconscious before him. Then he put him into the big leather sack he had with him and clapped the handcuffs on his wrists and the irons on his feet. The face of the dead man being invisible, Thoutii's stratagem was to pass off the corpse as his own. He ordered two hundred of his soldiers to conceal themselves in half of the four hundred jars he had brought with him, and filled the remainder with the ropes and wooden shackles; then he sealed them, corded them, and gave them to as many strong soldiers, saying, "Go quickly and tell the Prince of Joppa's equerry that I am slain. Let him go and tell his mistress, the Princess of Joppa, that Thoutii is conquered, that she may open the city gates to receive the dead body of the vanquished and the jars of booty that have been taken from him."

A relief showing prisoners of war brought back to Egypt as slaves, from Abu Simbel.

The equerry received this message and ran to tell the joyful news to his mistress. The gates of the town were opened, and Thoutii's men carried the jars containing the other soldiers into the town. Then they released their companions, and the whole Egyptian force fell upon the inhabitants of the city, capturing and binding them.

After he had rested, Thoutii sent a message to Pharaoh saying, "I have killed the Prince of Joppa and all the people of Joppa are prisoners. Let them be sent for and brought to Egypt, that your house may be filled with male and female slaves who will be yours for ever. Let Amen-Ra, thy father, the god of gods, be glorified."

CHAPTER VI

TALES OF MAGIC

THE TALE OF NEBKA AND THE CROCODILE

This tale and the two that follow represent part of a cycle of tales connected with Pharaoh Khufu of the Fourth Dynasty. The papyrus in which the stories survive dates from the Hyksos period, and lacks both its beginning and its end. Though two of the tales have clear moral overtones, they were apparently recorded as pure entertainment.

Khufu, or Kheops, the famous builder of the great pyramid at Gizeh, gathered his sons and his councillors around him and asked if any of them were aware of a man who could recount to him tales of the magicians. His son Khafra, in reply, stated that he was aware of one such tale, which had been handed down from the days of the king's forefather Nebka, and that it dealt with what occurred when Nebka visited the temple of Ptah of Ankhtaui.

Whilst proceeding to the temple, Nebka turned aside to visit his chief reciter, Uba-aner. He was followed by his retinue, among whom was a certain page, with whom Uba-aner's wife fell in love. She sent her servant to him with a present of a chest full of beautiful clothes. They met clandestinely in a summer-house or pavilion in the garden of Uba-aner, where they drank wine and made merry. But the steward of the house considered it his duty to inform his master of these happenings, and Uba-aner, being a man versed in magic, resolved to avenge himself thereby.

He called for his casket of ebony and electrum, and when they had brought it he fashioned a crocodile of wax of the length of seven fingers, and he laid a spell upon it; and toward evening the page went to the lake, which was in the garden, to bathe, whereupon acting on his master's instructions, the steward threw in the waxen crocodile behind him. At once it became a great crocodile, seven cubits in length and, opening its horrid jaws, seized on the page and dragged him under.

During this time the king had been staying with Uba-aner, and at the end of seven days he went forth again. As he was about to leave the house Uba-aner requested him to come and see the marvel that had happened. They went to the lake-side, and the reciter called upon the crocodile, which at once arose from the water holding the page.

A toy crocodile from ancient Egypt. Small figures of humans or animals, made of wood or clay and often with articulated joints, were common. A crocodile with moving jaws would have reminded the child of one of the most feared animals in Egypt.

The Great Pyramid of Khufu (Kheops) at Gizeh (opposite) is one of the most impressive sights of Ancient Egypt. With its outer layer of fine Tura limestone, subsequently removed by invaders for use as a building material, the pyramid originally stood 140 metres high.

"O king," said Uba-aner, "whatever I desire this crocodile to do, he will do." The king requested that the animal should be returned to the water; but Uba-aner lifted the crocodile in his hand, and straightway it turned to wax again. He then acquainted the king with what had passed between the page and his wife, and the monarch indignantly ordered the crocodile once more to seize the page, which it immediately did, plunging into the water with its prey and disappearing for ever. Nebka then commanded that the wife of Uba-aner be brought forth and that she be burned with fire and her ashes cast into the river.

So pleased was Khufu with this story that he ordered that the spirit of Nebka should be presented with a thousand loaves, a hundred draughts of beer, an ox, and two jars of incense, and that the ka of Uba-aner should receive a loaf, a jar of beer, a jar of incense, and a portion of meat.

THE PARTING OF THE WATERS

Another of Khufu's sons then told of a marvellous happening that came to pass in the days of King Seneferu.

Seneferu, feeling extremely bored and jaded, sought in every apartment of his palace for something with which to amuse himself, but in vain; so he called for Zazamankh, his chief reciter and scribe of the rolls, to whom he told his predicament. Zazamankh advised that the king should command that a boat be made ready, and that he should go upon the lake of the palace and be rowed to and fro upon its glassy surface by the royal ladies. He asked for twenty oars of ebony inlaid with gold, with blades of light wood inlaid with electrum. These were to be rowed by twenty ladies.

The king's heart was gladdened by the exercise; but one of the ladies who was steering lost a jewel of malachite from her hair. Immediately she ceased her singing, and so did her companions, and they ceased to row.

Seneferu inquired the reason, and they replied, "The steerswoman rows not."

The king then turned to the lady who had lost her jewel and asked her why she did not row.

"Alas!" she replied, "my jewel of malachite has fallen in the water, and my heart is sad."

The king bade her be of good cheer and said that he would replace it; but she childishly replied that she wanted her own piece of malachite back in its setting.

The king then called for Zazamankh and acquainted him with the circumstance which had befallen. Zazamankh then uttered a powerful spell, and behold! one part of the waters of the lake was piled upon the other, so that far below them the king and the rowers could see the jewel lying upon a piece of potsherd (fragment of pottery). Zazamankh descended from the boat and secured the jewel and brought it back to its owner, after which he once more commanded the waters to return to the place whence they came.

This surprising act lightened the hearts of the entire company, so that they spent a joyful afternoon, and Zazamankh was richly rewarded for his magical skill.

A statue of the Fifth Dynasty scribe Kha-f-Ra. Scribes were highly regarded professionals in Egypt.

A jewel from the tomb of Tutankhamun.
Egyptian jewellery often demonstrated
a very high level of craftsmanship,
and would have been highly prized
by its owners.

Kheops was so pleased with this tale that he commanded that the spirit of Seneferu should receive an offering similar to what had been presented to Nebka, and that the ka of Zazamankh should have presented to it a loaf, a jar of beer, and a jar of incense.

THE PROPHECY OF DEDI

The third surviving story of the sons of Khufu is incomplete, and is presented here in part only. The final surviving section, and the continuation now lost, apparently describe the unsuccessful efforts of Khufu himself to forestall the prophecy of the magician Dedi concerning his succession. The plain message is that the acceptance of fate is the course of wisdom.

But a third son told the king that, so far from recounting tales concerning persons of bygone times, he could tell him a magical story of a man who lived in his own days.

His name was Dedi, and he dwelt at Dedsneferu. He was one-hundred-

Small earthenware jars and bottles, symbolic containers of foodstuffs and personal supplies, such as incense that the deceased might need in the afterlife, are among the most common finds in Egyptian tombs.

A felucca sailing on the Nile. The Nile felucca is one of the oldest traditional sailing craft in the world, and has many similarities to the sailing craft of Ancient Egypt.

and-ten years old, and he ate daily five hundred loaves of bread and a side of beef, and drank a hundred draughts of beer. So great was his magical learning that if the head of a man or an animal were smitten off, Dedi could restore the deceased to life. He could tame wild beasts, and knew the designs of the House of Thoth. This design the king, Khufu, might like to know, and it would perhaps be of use to him in the construction of his pyramid.

Khufu at once ordered his son to bring this Dedi before him, and the prince, whose name was Hordedef, took a ship up the Nile to where the venerable magician dwelt. He was carried in a litter to the house of Dedi, whom he found lying on a couch at the door of his house, being massaged by his servants.

Hordedef told him that he had come from afar to bring him before his father, Khufu. Dedi replied with the salutation of praise, and together they went toward the ship that had brought the prince thither. Dedi asked that he might be given a boat and that his servants and his books might be brought to him. He was provided with two boats, in which these were stowed, and Dedi himself sat in the barge of the prince.

They duly reached the palace, where Hordedef announced to the king that he had brought the ancient sorcerer. The Pharoah at once gave orders that he should be led before him, and when he came asked how it was that he had not before heard of him. The sorcerer replied, "He cometh only who is called; the king calleth me, and behold I come."

Khufu said to him, "Is it true, as is said of thee, that if the head is smitten off a man or an animal, thou canst restore either to life?" Dedi

A fine wall-painting of a goose,
from Meydum, some 50 kilometres
up the Nile from Cairo.

replied that he could indeed perform such a feat of magic.

The king then requested that a prisoner be brought to him, but Dedi begged that a man should not be used for this purpose, saying, "Behold, we do thus not even to our cattle." A duck was then brought to him and decapitated, and its body was laid on the west side of the hall, and its head on the east side. Dedi then spoke some magic words, and lo! the body and the head of the bird approached each other and joined, and the duck stood up and quacked. Dedi then performed the same feat with a goose and an ox. Khufu, delighted with the success of these experiments, then asked Dedi if he knew of the designs of the House of Thoth. The magician replied that he did not know their number, but that he knew where they were. Pharaoh then asked him their hiding-place, and was told that in a chamber in Heliopolis, called the Plan-room, was a chest of whetstone in which the plans were concealed, Dedi adding, "O king, it is not I that shall bring them to thee."

"Who, then," asked Khufu, "shall bring them to me?"

And Dedi replied, "The eldest of the three children of Rud-didet shall bring them to thee."

"And who is Rud-didet?" asked Khufu.

"She is," replied Dedi, "the wife of a priest of Ra, lord of Sakhebu. But these three sons of hers are the sons of Ra the god, who has promised her that they shall reign over all this land, and that the eldest of them shall be high-priest in Heliopolis."

At this the king's heart was much troubled, and Dedi, seeing that he was in fear of the future, said to him, "Be not afraid because of what I have said, O king; for thy son shall reign, and thy son's son, before Rud-didet's sons shall rule the land; and behold! this progeny of Ra is not yet born."

Khufu then ordered that the sorcerer should be given a place in the palace of Hordedef, and be daily provided with a thousand loaves, a hundred draughts of beer, an ox, and a hundred bunches of onions.

Traditional loaves of bread from
a bakery at Luxor.

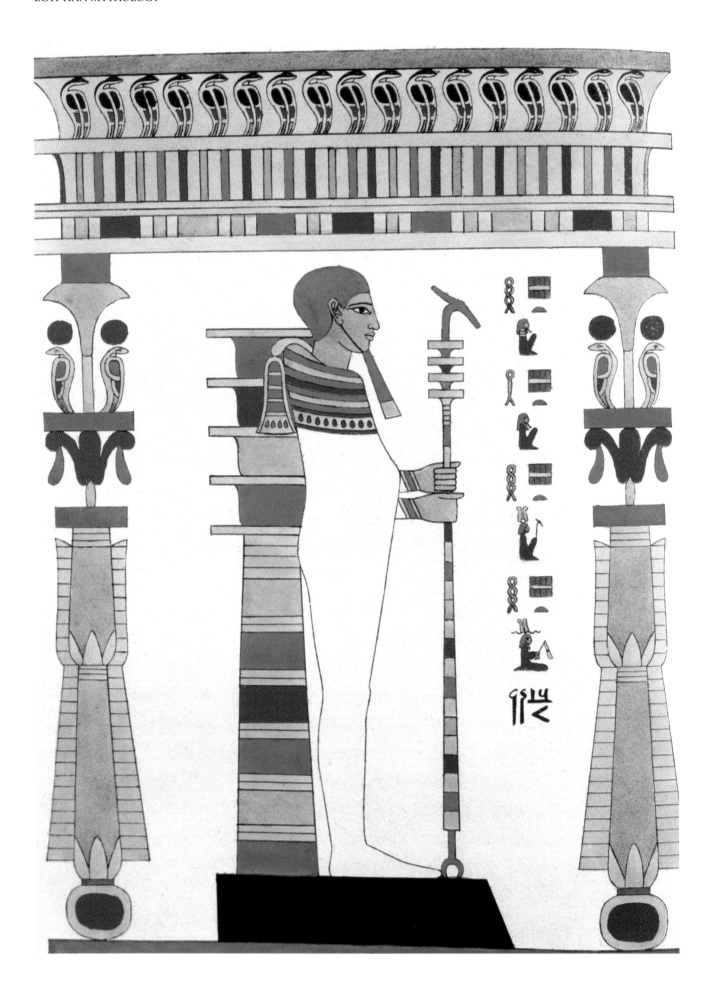

THE TALE OF SETNE

The historical son of Ramesses II, Setne the High Priest of Ptah, is here recognized as a magician. His success in winning a book of magic spells from the spirit of a dead magician leads him to disaster. This tale survives in a fragmentary papyrus in Cairo dating from the Ptolemaic period.

The prince and magician Setne was conversing on one occasion with one of Pharoah's wise men who appeared sceptical of his powers. In reply to his strictures upon the efficacy of magic Setne offered to take him to a place where he would find a book possessed of magical powers written by Thoth himself, and containing two potent spells, the first of which was capable of enchanting the entire universe, and so powerful that all animals and birds and fishes could be commanded by it. The second enabled a man in the tomb to see Ra rising in heaven with his cycle of gods; the Moon rising with all the stars of heaven; the fishes in the depths of the ocean.

The wise man thereupon very naturally requested Setne to tell him the repository of this marvellous volume, and learned that it was in the tomb of Nefer-ka-Ptah at Memphis. Thence Setne proceeded, accompanied by his brother, and passed three days and nights in seeking for the tomb of Nefer-ka-Ptah, which he eventually discovered.

He uttered some magical words over it, the earth opened, and they descended to the chamber where the actual tomb was situated. The book, which lay in the sarcophagus, illuminated the place so brilliantly that they required no torches, and by its light they perceived in the grave not only its original inhabitant, but his wife and son, who, though they were buried at Coptos, had come in their ka-shapes to reside with their husband and father. Setne informed them that he desired to remove the book, but Ahura, the wife of Nefer-ka-Ptah, earnestly requested him not to do so, and informed him how its possession had already proved unfortunate to others.

Her husband, she said, had given up most of his time to the study of magic, and for the price of a hundred pieces of silver and two elaborate sarcophagi had bought from the priest of Ptah the secret of the hiding-place of the wonderful volume. The book was contained in an iron chest sunk in

A painting of Ptah (opposite), patron god of handicrafts and metalwork. Setne, son of Ramesses II, was a high priest of this god.

The extraordinary fertility of the lands bordering the Nile has always supported a wide variety of birds. Many of those which can be seen today can be identified in Egyptian paintings.

An elaborately decorated box from the Museum of Antiquities, Cairo. The nested boxes containing the magic book sought by Setne recall the nested sarcophagi found in Egyptian tombs.

The serpent-god Nef or Neheb was a deity of the underworld reminiscent of the world-serpent found in other mythologies. The story of Nefer-ka-Ptah's struggle with the serpent protector of the book of spells would have had great mythological resonance for the Egyptians.

the middle of the river at Coptos; in the iron box was a bronze box; in the bronze box a box of palm-tree wood, which again contained a box of ebony and ivory, in which was a silver box, which lastly contained a gold box, the true receptacle of the book. Swarms of serpents and noxious reptiles of all kinds guarded the volume, and round it was coiled a serpent which could not die.

Nefer-ka-Ptah, with his wife and child, set out for Coptos, where he obtained from the high-priest a model of a floating raft and figures of workmen provided with the necessary tools. Over these he recited words of power, so that they became alive. Shortly afterward they located the box, and by further magical formulae Nefer-ka-Ptah put the reptiles which surrounded it to flight. Twice he slew the great serpent which lay coiled round the chest of iron, but each time it came to life again. The third time, however, he cut it in two, and laid sand between the two pieces, so that they might not again join together.

Opening the various boxes, he took out the mysterious volume which they had contained, and read the first spell upon its pages. This acquainted him with all the secrets of heaven and earth. He perused the second and saw the sun rising in the heavens, with all the accompanying gods. His wife followed his example with similar results. Nefer-ka-Ptah then copied the spells on a piece of papyrus, on which he sprinkled incense, dissolved the whole in water, and drank it, thus making certain that the knowledge of the formula would remain with him for ever.

A Game of Draughts with the Dead

But the god Thoth was angry with him for what he had done, and acquainted Ra with this sacrilegious act. Ra at once decided that Nefer-ka-Ptah, and his wife and child, should never return to Memphis; and whilst returning to Coptos, Ahura and her son fell into the river and were drowned. Shortly afterward Nefer-ka-Ptah himself met a like fate.

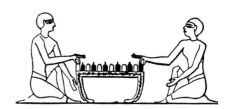

Egyptians playing a game of draughts. Other boardgames such as backgammon are also thought to have their origins in Ancient Egypt.

This story, however, did not deter Setne, who had made up his mind to possess the book. The disembodied Nefer-ka-Ptah proposed that its ownership should be settled by playing a game of draughts, the winner to retain the volume. To this Setne agreed. Nefer-ka-Ptah did his best to win, first honestly, and then by fraud, but in the end he lost the game.

Setne requested his brother, who had accompanied him into the mausoleum, to ascend to the place above and bring him the magical writings. This was done, and the spells were worked upon Setne, who grasped the wonderful book of Thoth and ascended to heaven with marvellous swiftness.

As he departed, however, Nefer-ka-Ptah remarked to his wife that he would soon make him return. The prophecy of Ahura that Setne would be unlucky if he persisted in keeping the volume was indeed fully borne out. He was tormented by a beautiful succubus who succeeded not only in seducing him into transferring all his property to her, but also in persuading him to kill his own children in order to guarantee the transfer. Such were his troubles that the Pharaoh commanded him to return the book to the keeping of Nefer-ka-Ptah.

THE TRUE HISTORY OF SETNE AND HIS SON SE-OSIRIS

This long tale of the son of the magician Setne survives in a papyrus in the British Museum, dating from the Ptolemaic period. It contains a description of the other world which reflects the details given in the *Book of the Dead*, and the magic duel that forms its climax reveals in passing the prejudices of the inhabitants of Lower Egypt against the inhabitants of the upper Nile.

Once upon a time there was a king called Ousimares, and he had a son called Setne. This son was a scribe; he was clever with his hands, indeed in all things, and he excelled in all the learned arts of Egypt.

It happened that the chiefs of certain foreign lands sent a message to Pharaoh challenging him to a contest of wisdom. If an Egyptian wise man could answer the puzzle they had set, then these chiefs would acknowledge the inferiority of their country to Egypt; but if, on the other hand, neither scribe nor wise man in Egypt could accomplish it, then they would proclaim the inferiority of Egypt. Now Ousimares called his son Setne and repeated these words to him, and immediately Setne gave the answer to the puzzle, so that the latter were forced to carry out the conditions and admit the superiority of Egypt. And thus were they robbed of their triumph, so great was the wisdom of Setne, and none other ever dared again to send such messages to Pharaoh.

The god Imhotep, historically the chief minister of Djoser and architect of the Step Pyramid, was venerated by later Egyptians as a god of learning and medicine.

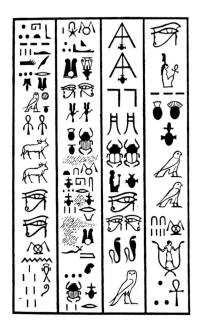

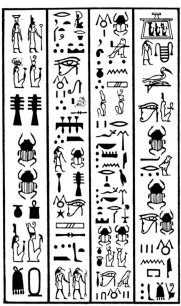

Amulets – portable inscriptions or scrolls of verses or spells to ward off evil – were intended to be carried at all times. These two are from a sequence of 104 associated with Osiris.

Now Setne and his wife Mahîtouaskhît were greatly grieved, for they had no son. One day, when he was troubled more than usual over this, his wife went to the temple of Imhotep, and she prayed before him, saying, "Turn thy face to me, O Imhotep, son of Ptah, thou who workest miracles, who art beneficent in all thy doings. It is thou who canst give a son to those who are sonless. Oh, hear my prayer, and grant that I shall bear a son!"

And that night Mahîtouaskhît slept in the temple, and there she dreamed a dream wherein she was directed to prepare a magical remedy, and told that by this means her desire for a son should be fulfilled. On waking she did all according to her dream, and in time she and Setne conceived a child. Setne told Pharaoh with great joy, while to his wife, for her protection, he gave an amulet and put spells about her.

And one night Setne dreamed, and a voice said to him, "Mahîtouaskhît, thy wife, will bring forth a son, and through him many wonders shall be accomplished in the land of Egypt. And the name of thy son shall be Se-Osiris." When Setne awoke and remembered these words he rejoiced and was glad in heart.

Se-Osiris

In due time a son was born, and according to the dream he was called Se-Osiris. And the child developed rapidly beyond all other children, and Setne loved him so greatly that scarce an hour passed without his seeing him. In time he was put to school, but soon showed that he knew more than the tutor could teach him. He began to read the magical papyri with the priestly scribes in the "Double House of Life" of the temple of Ptah, and all those about him were lost in astonishment. Then Setne was so pleased that he brought his son before Pharaoh at a festival, so that all the magicians of the king might compete in wisdom against him and have to acknowledge their defeat.

While Setne and his son Se-Osiris were preparing for the festival, loud voices of lamentation rose upon the air, and Setne, looking forth from the terrace of his apartments, saw the body of a rich man being carried to the

The unfinished tomb of Ramose, a vizier and governor of Thebes. Many Egyptians even of moderate wealth were able to make arrangements for elaborate tombs and funerary rites, frequently including full mummification.

An alabaster sphinx from Memphis, the capital during the Old Kingdom. Memphis lies today within the suburbs of Cairo, and the mountains visited by Setne are the hills that surround the city.

mountains for burial with great honour and loud wailing. Again he looked forth, and this time he saw the body of a peasant borne along wrapped in a mat of straw and without a soul to mourn him. And seeing this Setne exclaimed, "By the life of Osiris, god of Amenti, may it be that I come into Amenti as this rich man comes, honoured and lamented, and not as the peasant, alone and already forgotten!"

Upon hearing this Se-Osiris said, "Nay, my father, rather may the fate of the poor man be thine, and not that of the rich one!"

Setne was astonished and hurt at this and cried, "Are they the words of a son who loves his father?"

Se-Osiris answered him: "My father, I will show to thee each in his place, the peasant unwept and the rich man so lamented."

A Vision of Amenti

Then Setne demanded of him how he could accomplish this. The child Se-Osiris began to recite words from the magical books, words of power. Next he took his father by the hand and led him to an unknown place in the mountains of Memphis.

Here there were seven great halls filled with people of all conditions. They traversed three of these without hindrance. Upon entering the fourth, Setne saw a mass of men who rushed hither and thither, writhing as creatures attacked them from behind; others, famished, were springing and jumping in their efforts to reach food which was suspended above them, whilst other creatures dug holes at their feet to prevent them attaining their object. In the fifth hall were venerable spirits who had each found their proper and fitting place, while those who were accused of crimes lingered kneeling at the door, which pivoted upon the eye of a man who ceaselessly prayed and groaned.

In the sixth hall were the gods of Amenti, who sat in council, each in his place, whilst the keepers of the portals called out the causes. In the seventh hall was seated the great god Osiris on a golden throne, crowned with his plumed diadem. On his left was Anubis, and on his right the god Thoth. In the midst were the scales wherein were weighed the faults and virtues of the souls of the dead, while Thoth wrote down the judgment that Anubis pronounced.

Then those whose faults outweighed their virtues were delivered to Amait, the attendant of the Lord of Amenti; their souls and bodies were destroyed for ever. But those whose virtues were greater than their failings took their place among the gods and spirits, and there their souls found a heaven. Those, again, whose merits and faults were equal were put amongst the servitors of Sekerosiris.

Then Setne saw near the place of Osiris one of exalted rank, robed in the finest linen. And while Setne was marvelling at all he had seen in the land of Amenti, Se-Osiris, his little son, said unto him, "My father Setne, seest thou that great personage in fine robes and near to Osiris? That peasant whom thou didst see carried out of Memphis without a soul to

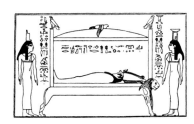

The falcon-headed Seker-Osiris laid out on a bier between Isis and Nephthys. Seker-Osiris was a deity combining attributes of Osiris with those of Seker, the other major deity of the underworld. He was lord of the Egyptian version of Purgatory.

Images of labourers carrying out the task of brickmaking. Though much Egyptian mythology involves aristocratic characters, Ancient Egypt had a large working population who shared the religious concerns of their rulers.

accompany him, and his body wrapped in a mat, dost thou remember, my father? Well, that peasant is the one beside Osiris! When he had come to Amenti and they weighed his faults and virtues, lo! his virtues outweighed all. And by the judgment of the gods all the honours that had been the share of the rich man were given to the peasant, and by the law of Osiris he takes his place amidst the honoured and exalted. But the rich man, when he had come to Hades and his merits were weighed, lo! his faults weighed heavier, and he is that man you have seen upon whose eye pivots the door of the fifth hall, the man who cries and prays aloud with great agony. By the life of Osiris, god of Amenti, if upon earth I said to thee, 'Rather may the fate of the peasant be thine than that of the rich man,' it was because I knew their fates, my father."

And Setne answered and said, "My son Se-Osiris, numberless marvels have I seen in Amenti; but tell me the meaning of those people we saw rushing before creatures who devoured them, and the others ever trying to reach the food beyond their reach."

Se-Osiris answered him: "In truth, my father, they are under the curse of the gods; they are those who upon earth wasted their substance, and the creatures who devour them without ceasing are the women with whom they squandered both life and substance, and now they have naught, though they work day and night. And so it is with all: as they have been on earth, so it is with them in Amenti, according to their good and bad deeds. That is the immutable law of the gods, the law that knows no change and under which all men must come when they enter the afterlife."

Then Setne and his son returned hand in hand from the mountains of

A formal audience, recreated from an original Egyptian painting. In this case the god Amen Ra (seated), attended by the god Khonsu and the goddess Maat, receives the kneeling Ramesses II in the presence of his father Seti I (left).

Memphis. A fear was upon Setne because of Se-Osiris, who remained silent, and so he pronounced words that exorcize the ghosts of the dead. Always afterward he remembered all he had seen, and marvelled at it, but spoke of it to no man.

And when Se-Osiris was twelve years of age there was no scribe or magician in Memphis who was his equal in the reading of the magical books.

The Reading of the Sealed Letter

After this it happened one day that the Pharaoh Ousimares was seated in the Hall of Audience with the princes, the military chiefs, and the nobles of Egypt, each according to his rank, gathered about him. One said unto Pharaoh, "Here is a rascally Ethiopian who would fain have speech with you, and who carries a sealed letter." And Pharaoh commanded that the man be brought before him. And when he was come he made obeisance and said, "Here is a sealed letter which I bear, and I would fain know if amongst your wise men there any who can read its contents without breaking the seals. If, O king, you have not such a one among your scribes and magicians, I shall take back to my country, the land of the Negro, the story of Egypt's failure and inferiority."

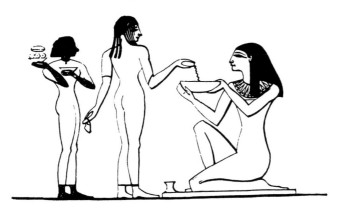

An Egyptian noblewoman being waited on by a black and a white slave. Egyptian cultural contact with black Africa, particularly Ethiopia, was extensive.

Upon hearing these words all were amazed, and those about the king exclaimed loudly, while Pharaoh bade some bring to him his son Setne. When he had come, instantly obeying the royal command and bowing low before him, Pharaoh said, "My son Setne, hast thou heard the words of this insolent Ethiopian?" and then he repeated the challenge.

Setne was astonished, but he answered immediately, "Great Lord, who can read a letter without its being opened and spread before him? But if you will give me ten days, I will think upon it and do what I can to avoid the report of Egypt's failure being carried to the Negroes, eaters of gum."

And Pharaoh said, "Those days are granted, my son." Then rooms were appointed for the Ethiopian, and Pharaoh rose from his palace sad at heart and went fasting to his couch.

And Setne, pondering and much disturbed, threw himself upon his couch, but knew no rest. His wife Mahîtouaskhît came to him and would fain have shared his trouble, but he said that it was not for a woman to share or one that she might help him in. Later his son Se-Osiris came and begged to know what so sorely troubled his father, and again Setne refused to speak, saying that it was not for a child. But the boy persisted, and at last Setne told him of the challenge of the Ethiopian. The moment he had finished Se-Osiris laughed, and his father asked the reason of his mirth.

"My father," he answered, "I laugh to see you there, so troubled in heart because of such a small affair. I will read that letter of the Ethiopian, read it all without breaking the seals."

Hearing this, Setne rose instantly. "But what proof can you give me of the truth of what you say, my son?"

Se-Osiris answered, "My father, go thou to the lower floor of this house and take what books you please from their place. As you do so I shall read that which you have taken from its place while I stand before you."

And it happened as Se-Osiris had said. Each book that his father lifted the boy read without its being opened. Setne then lost no time in acquainting Pharaoh with all that Se-Osiris had done, and so lightened was the heart of the king that he made a great feast in honour of Setne and his young son.

After this Pharaoh sent for the Ethiopian. And when he entered the Hall of Audience he was placed in the midst of all, and the young Se-Osiris took up his place beside him. But first the boy put a curse upon the man and his gods if he should dare to say falsely that what he read was not true. And seeing the boy, the Ethiopian prostrated himself before him in fear. Then Se-Osiris began to read the letter with its seals still unbroken, and all heard his voice. And the words were:

The Contents of the Letter

"It happened during the reign of the Pharaoh Manakhphrê-Siamon, who was a beneficent ruler and in whose time the land overflowed with all good things, who endowed the temples richly, that when the King of Nubia was taking his rest in the pleasure-house of Amen he overheard the voices of three Ethiopians who were talking behind the house. One of them was speaking in a high voice, saying, among other things, that if the god Amen would preserve him from the enmity of the King of Egypt he could put a spell on the people of that country so that a great darkness should reign and they should not see the moon for three days and three nights.

"Then the second man said that if Amen would guard him he would cause the Pharaoh to be transported to the land of the Negroes, and there, before the king of that country and in public, he should suffer five hundred blows, and afterward he should be taken back to his country in not more than six hours.

"After this the third man spoke, saying that if Amen would preserve him he would then send a blight upon the land of Egypt, a blight for the space of three years. When the king heard this he ordered that these three men be brought before him. He said unto them, 'Which of you said that he would cause that the people of Egypt should not see the moon for three days and three nights?' And they answered that it was Horus son of Tririt (the sow).

"Again the king said, 'Which of you said that he had power to cause the King of Egypt to be brought hither?' And they answered that it was Horus son of Tnahsit (the negress).

The god Amen, shown here in his manifestation as Amen-Ra, is always recognizable by his tall headdress.

"Again the king said, 'Which of you said that he would cause a blight to fall upon Egypt?' And they answered that it was Horus son of Triphît (the princess).

"Then the king bade Horus son of Tnahsit come near, and he said to him, 'By Amen, the Bull of Meroe, if thou canst accomplish what thou hast said then rich rewards shall be thine.'

"And Horus son of Tnahsit fashioned a litter and four bearers of wax. Over them he chanted magical words, he breathed upon them and gave them life, and finally he bade them wend their way to Egypt and bring back the king of that land in order that he might suffer five hundred blows from the kourbash before the King of the Negroes."

Here Se-Osiris paused and, turning to the Ethiopian, said, "The curse of Amen fall upon thee! These words that I have said, are they not written in the letter thou holdest in thine hand?"

And the rascally Ethiopian bowed low before him, saying, "They are written there, my lord!"

Then Se-Osiris resumed his magical reading: "And all happened as Horus son of Tnahsit had devised. By the power of sorcery Pharaoh was taken to the land of the Negroes, and there suffered five hundred blows of the kourbash. After that he was carried back to Egypt, as had been said, and, wakening the next morning in the temple of the god Horus, he lay in great pain, his body sorely bruised.

"Bewildered, he asked his courtiers how such could have happened in Egypt. They, thinking some madness had fallen upon their king, and yet ashamed of their thoughts, spoke soothingly to him, and said that the great gods would heal his afflictions. But still they asked him the meaning of his strange words, and suddenly he remembered all that had happened to him and recounted it to his courtiers."

Pharaoh Horemheb carried on a sedan chair, preceded by a priest and three Nubian slaves. The kingdom of Nubia maintained an uneasy relationship with Egypt for most of their history.

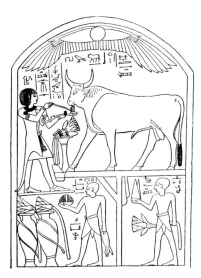

The sacred bull of Meroe, shown here, was regarded as another manifestation of Amen.

An extraordinary image of an Egyptian magician, reproduced from an earthenware amulet.

Magic Versus Magic

"When they saw his bruised body they made a great clamour. And then Pharaoh sent for his chief magician and he at once cried out that the evil and affliction of the king were due to the sorceries of the Ethiopians.

"'By the life of Ptah,' he continued, 'I shall bring them to torture and execution.' And Pharaoh bade him make all speed, lest the magic of the Ethiopians should carry him off again the next night. The chief magician carried his secret books and amulets to the place where Pharaoh lay, and chanted above him magical words and incantations. Then, with many gifts, he embarked in a boat and made haste to reach the temple of Khmounon, and there he prayed to the god Thoth that all evil should be averted from Pharaoh and the land of Egypt. And that night he slept in the temple, and he dreamed a dream in which the god Thoth appeared to him and instructed him in divine magic that would preserve the king from the wiles of the Ethiopians.

"On waking the magician remembered all, and without losing a moment fulfilled all that he had been told in his dream. And then he wrote the charm to preserve Pharaoh from all sorcery. On the second day the Ethiopians endeavoured to renew their enchantments, but all was now unavailing against the person of Pharaoh. The third morning Pharaoh recounted to his chief musicians all that had happened during the night, and how the Ethiopians had failed in their attempts.

"Then the Egyptian magician fashioned a litter and four bearers of

Elaborate relief-carvings and inscriptions on an Egyptian amulet intended to protect the bearer against the bite of the black scorpion.

wax. He put a spell upon them and breathed life into them, bidding them go and bring before Pharaoh the King of the Negroes, that he might suffer five hundred blows upon his body and then be carried back to his own land again. And the waxen figures promised to do all the magician had commanded."

Again Se-Osiris paused, and again he demanded of the Ethiopian if his words were not the words of the sealed letter. And the Ethiopian bowed low to the ground, saying they were the words in very truth. Se-Osiris began again to read the hidden words:

"And as it happened to Pharaoh, so was the fate of the King of the Negroes, who awoke sorely bruised in the morning following. He called loudly for his courtiers, and when they saw the state of their king they made a great clamour. Again he called and commanded that Horus son of Tnahsit, be brought before him. When he had come the king upbraided him, and commanded him to go to Egypt and there learn how to save him from the sorceries of Pharaoh's chief magician.

"But no spell devised by the Ethiopian could preserve the king from the magic of the Egyptians, and three times he was carried to that country and humiliated, whilst his body was in great pain, so sorely bruised was it. Then he cursed Horus son of Tnahsit, and threatened him with a slow and dreadful death unless he could preserve him from Pharaoh's vengeance.

"Then in fear and trouble Horus went to his mother Tnahsit and told her all, and that he must go to Egypt to see the one who had worked these powerful sorceries and endeavour to inflict upon him a fitting punishment. And his mother Tnahsit, on hearing this, warned him against coming into the presence Pharaoh's chief magician, for he would never prevail against him. But he answered that he must go.

"Then she arranged with him that by signs and signals between them he should let her know how he fared, and if he were in danger, then she should try to save him. And he promised, saying that if he were vanquished, then whatever she ate, whatever she drank, and the sky above should turn to the colour of blood."

The litter with four bearers conjured up by the Egyptian magician was clearly a familiar mode of transport for the nobility: here a military commander uses such a litter, with an attendant carrying a kind of parasol.

The War of Enchantments

Hieroglyphics, from the tomb of Ramesses I at Luxor. This system of picture writing emerged around 3000 BC. At first each picture indicated an object, but as the system developed the pictures were also used to represent sounds.

"And after this he journeyed to Egypt, seeking the magician whose sorceries had prevailed against his own. He penetrated to the Royal Hall of Audience and came before Pharaoh, crying in a high voice, 'Who is it among you who is putting spells upon me?'

"And Pharaoh's chief magician called out in answer, saying, 'Ha! Ethiopian, is it thou who workedst evil against Pharaoh?' Horus son of

Tnahsit cried out in great anger, and by a spell he caused a great flame to rise from the midst of the hall, at which Pharaoh and the Egyptians cried out to the chief of the magicians to save them. Then by his power the chief magician caused a shower of rain to fall so that the flame was extinguished.

"Again the Ethiopian wrought his magic, causing a great darkness to fall upon them all so that the people could not see each other, but this also was dispersed by the magician of the Egyptians. Then followed more machinations by Horus son of Tnahsit, but each time was he vanquished.

"At last he asked for mercy, and vowed before the gods that never again would he trouble Egypt or Pharaoh. They gave him a boat and sent him back to his own land. So were the sorceries of the Ethiopians rendered as naught."

With this Se-Osiris finished the reading of the sealed letter. And then he began to reveal to all there – Pharaoh, the princes, and the nobles – that the Ethiopian now before them was none other than that Horus son of Tnahsit, returned after five hundred years to trouble Egypt and its king again. But against this day he himself, Se-Osiris, had been born again, for he was that former chief magician of the Pharaoh Manakhphrê come back once more to protect Egypt and Pharaoh from the wiles of the Ethiopians.

And with these words he caused a great flame to consume the Ethiopian, there in the midst of the Hall of Audience, so that not a vestige of the creature remained. But afterward, when they looked for Se-Osiris, they found that he too had disappeared like a shadow from before Pharaoh and his father Setne, and neither of them ever saw him again.

At these happenings everyone marvelled, and Pharaoh said that Se-Osiris was the wisest and most wonderful of all magicians, and that never again would the world see his like.

But the hearts of Setne and his wife were heavy, and they grieved sorely for their son Se-Osiris. Then comfort came to them, for again the wife of Setne bore a son, and they called him Ousimanthor. And so the heart of Setne was glad, and he made offerings in the name of Se-Osiris in remembrance.

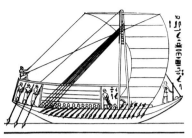

Large Egyptian boats, like that used to return the Ethiopian magician to his native land, combined sail and oar-power. Because timber was always in short supply, the hulls of even the largest were made of huge quantities of papyrus reeds.

Princes of Egypt, travelling in style in lightly built two-horse chariots.

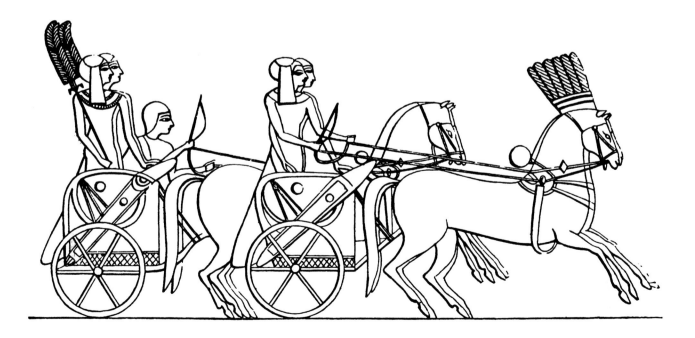

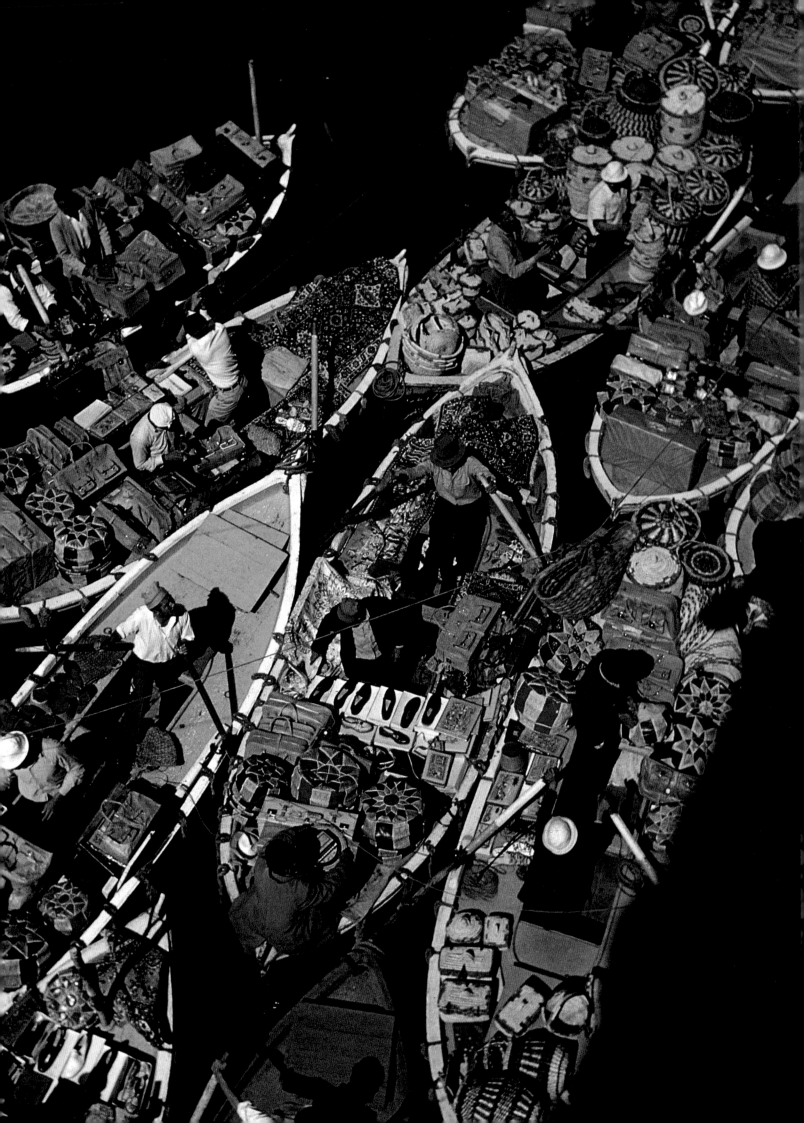

CHAPTER VII

FOLKTALES OF EGYPT

THE SHIPWRECKED SAILOR

This fantastic tale of a sole survivor of a shipwreck recalls the story of Sindbad. It was presented in the original in the form of a report, and survived in a papyrus in St Petersburg.

A wandering sailor, recounting his adventures to his superior officer, begs of him an introduction to Pharaoh. His master will not credit his story, but the man protests that it is true.

He was bound for the mines of the king, he says, and took ship on a vessel one-hundred-and-fifty cubits long and forty cubits wide, manned by one hundred of the best sailors of Egypt, whose hearts were stronger than lions, and who were inured to hardship and voyage. They laughed at the thought of tempests, but as they approached land a great wind arose and mighty waves dashed against the vessel.

The narrator seized upon a piece of timber, and not too soon, for the ship and all who remained in her were submerged. He floated for three days and then was cast on an island, where he crawled into the shadow of some bushes upon which grew figs and grapes. He also succeeded in finding melons, berries, and grain, and in snaring fishes and birds. Contented to remain there a while, he dug a pit and lighted a fire, and offered up a sacrifice to the gods.

All at once a terrible uproar like the rumbling of thunder surprised him out of his equanimity. At first he took it to be the noise of a tempest at sea, but shortly he perceived that the trees shook and that the earth had become violently agitated. Just before him lay a great serpent thirty cubits long, with a beard two cubits in length; its back was covered with scales of gold, and its body was the colour of lapis-lazuli.

Terrified, the sailor threw himself on his face before this monster, which regarded him for a moment with its terrible eyes, and then, opening its ponderous jaws, addressed him as follows: "What has brought thee to this island, little one? Speak quickly, and if thou dost not acquaint me with something I have not heard, or knew not before, thou shalt vanish like flame." Without giving the unfortunate mariner time to answer, it raised him in its jaws and carried him to its lair, where it laid him down gently enough,

The nomarch (provincial ruler) Khnemu-hetep spearing fish. The marshlands of the Nile delta provided ample opportunities for Egyptians to gain experience in catching fish and birds.

The history of maritime experience exemplified by these boats in modern Port Said (opposite) reaches back into the ancient Egyptian past, as the story of "The Shipwrecked Sailor" indicates.

129

safe and sound. Once more it demanded of him what power had brought him to that island, and the sailor, trembling in every limb, replied that on his way to the mines of Pharaoh he had been wrecked.

On hearing his tale the serpent told him to be of good cheer and not to be afraid; that God had brought him to a blessed island where nothing was lacking, and which was filled with all good things; that in four months' time a ship should come for him; that he should return into Egypt; and that he should die in his own town.

To cheer him up the benevolent monster described the island to him. Its population consisted of seventy-five serpents, young and old, and there these beings dwelt in harmony and plenty. The sailor on his part was none the less friendly, and in the goodness of his heart offered to recount to Pharaoh the presence and condition of the serpent island, promising to bring to the monster personally sacred oils and perfumes and the incense with which the gods were honoured. He would also slay asses for him in sacrifice, pluck birds for him, and bring him ships full of the treasures of Egypt.

In reply the serpent merely smiled at him indulgently and a little disdainfully. "Tell me not," he said, "that you are rich in perfumes, for I know that all you have is but ordinary incense. I am Prince of the Land of Punt and possess as much perfume as I require, and let me tell you that when you depart from this place you shall never behold it again, for it shall be changed into waves."

In due time the ship approached, as the serpent had prophesied, and in order to observe by what sort of company it was manned the sailor climbed into a high tree. As it neared the shore the serpent bade him farewell, and provided him with gifts of precious perfumes, sweet woods, cassia, kohl, incense, ivory tusks, apes, baboons, and all kinds of precious merchandise. Embarking with these, he was finally told by the genius of the island that in two months he should behold his wife and children. The rescued mariner then sailed through Nubia down the Nile to the residence of the Pharaoh, and the tale ends with the request on the part of its narrator that his captain should provide him with an escort so that he might present himself before the Pharaoh and recount his story.

Kohl was an important cosmetic, widely used as eye make-up in Egypt. It was imported, as is shown in this drawing of Asiatic foreigners bringing eye make-up to Khnemu-hetep II at Bani Hasan.

The cultivated strip of land either side of the Nile is extremely narrow in some places. The difficulty faced by the peasant in the following story cannot have been uncommon.

THE PEASANT AND THE WORKMAN

An apparently very popular tale, the following story survives in four separate papyri. The original text makes great stylistic play of the attempts of the peasant to speak in what he takes to be a refined and elaborate manner to the magistrate.

In the Salt Country there dwelt a *sekhti* (peasant) with his family. He made his living by trading with Henenseten in salt, natron, rushes, and the other products of his country, and as he journeyed thither he had to pass through the lands of the house of Fefa. Now there dwelt by the canal a man named Tehuti-nekht, the son of Asri, a serf to the High Steward Meruitensa. Tehuti-nekht had so far encroached on the path – for roads and paths were not protected by law in Egypt as in other countries – that there was but a narrow strip left, with the canal on one side and a cornfield on the other. When Tehuti-nekht saw the *sekhti* approaching with his burdened asses, his evil heart coveted the beasts and the goods they bore, and he called to the gods to open a way for him to steal the possessions of the *sekhti*.

This was the plan he conceived. "I will take," said he, "a shawl, and will spread it upon the path. If the *sekhti* drives his asses over it – and there is no other way – then I shall easily pick a quarrel with him." He had no sooner thought of the project than it was carried into effect. A servant, at Tehuti-nekht's bidding, fetched a shawl and spread it over the path so that one end was in the water, the other among the corn.

When the *sekhti* drew nigh he drove his asses over the shawl. He had no alternative.

"Hold!" cried Tehuti-nekht with well-simulated wrath, "surely you do not intend to drive your beasts over my clothes!"

"I will try to avoid them," responded the good-natured peasant, and he caused the rest of his asses to pass higher up, among the corn.

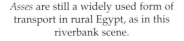

Asses are still a widely used form of transport in rural Egypt, as in this riverbank scene.

"Do you, then, drive your asses through my corn?" said Tehuti-nekht, more wrathfully than ever.

"There is no other way," said the harassed peasant. "You have blocked the path with your shawl, and I must leave the path."

While the two argued upon the matter one of the asses helped itself to a mouthful of corn, whereupon Tehuti-nekht's plaints broke out afresh.

"Behold!" he cried, "your ass is eating my corn. I will take your ass, and he shall pay for the theft."

"Shall I be robbed," cried the *sekhti*, "in the lands of the Lord Steward Meruitensa, who treateth robbers so hardly? Behold, I will go to him. He will not suffer this misdeed of thine."

"Thinkest thou he will hearken to thy plaint?" sneered Tehuti-nekht.

"Poor as thou art, who will concern himself with thy woes? Lo, I am the Lord Steward Meruitensa." And so saying he beat the *sekhti* sorely, stole all his asses and drove them into pasture.

In vain the *sekhti* wept and implored him to restore his property. Tehuti-nekht bade him hold his peace, threatening to send him to the Demon of Silence if he continued to complain. Nevertheless, the *sekhti* petitioned him for a whole day.

At length, finding that he was wasting his breath, the peasant betook himself to Henen-ni-sut, there to lay his case before the Lord Steward Meruitensa. On his arrival he found the latter preparing to embark in his boat, which was to carry him to the judgment-hall. The *sekhti* bowed himself to the ground, and told the Lord Steward that he had a grievance to lay before him, praying him to send one of his followers to hear the tale.

The Lord Steward granted the suppliant's request, and sent to him one from among his train. To the messenger the *sekhti* revealed all that had befallen him on his journey, the manner in which Tehuti-nekht had closed the path so as to force him on to the corn, and the cruelty with which he had beaten him and stolen his property. In due time these matters were told to the Lord Steward, who laid the case before the nobles who were with him in the judgment-hall.

"Let this *sekhti* bring a witness," they said, "and if he establish his case, it may be necessary to beat Tehuti-nekht, or perchance he will be made to pay a trifle for the salt and natron he has stolen."

The Lord Steward said nothing, and the *sekhti* himself came unto him and hailed him as the greatest of the great, the orphan's father, the widow's husband, the guide of the needy, and so on. Very eloquent was the *sekhti*, and in his florid speech he skillfully combined eulogy with his plea for justice, so that the Lord Steward was interested and flattered in spite of himself.

Now at that time there sat upon the throne of Egypt the King Neb-ka-n-ra, and to him came the Lord Steward Meruitensa, saying: "Behold, my lord, I have been sought by a *sekhti* whose goods were stolen. Most eloquent of mortals is he. What would my lord that I do unto him?"

"Do not answer his speeches," said the king, "but put his words in writing and bring them to us. See that he and his wife and children are supplied with meat and drink, but do not let him know who provides it."

The Lord Steward did as the king had commanded him. He gave to the peasant a daily ration of bread and beer, and to his wife sufficient corn to

Bread was a staple in Ancient Egypt. Here a drawing from a Fifth Dynasty tomb at Saqqara shows bakers at work.

Peasants reaping corn from a stele found near Hermopolis. Except for the failure of the annual Nile flood, Egypt generally achieved a surplus over its grain needs at harvest time.

feed herself and her children. But the *sekhti* knew not whence the provisions came.

A second time the peasant sought the judgment-hall and poured forth his complaint to the Lord Steward; and yet a third time he came, and the Lord Steward commanded that he be beaten with staves, to see whether he would desist. But no, the *sekhti* came a fourth, a fifth, a sixth time, endeavouring with pleasant speeches to open the ear of the judge. Meruitensa hearkened to him not at all, yet the *sekhti* did not despair, but came again unto the ninth time. And at the ninth time the Lord Steward sent two of his followers to the *sekhti*, and the peasant trembled exceedingly, for he feared that he was about to be beaten once more because of his importunity. The message, however, was a reassuring one. Meruitensa declared that he had been greatly delighted by the peasant's eloquence and would see that he obtained satisfaction. He then caused the *sekhti*'s petitions to be written on clean papyri and sent to the king, according as the monarch had commanded. Neb-ka-n-ra was also much pleased with the speeches, but the giving of judgment he left entirely in the hands of the Lord Steward.

Meruitensa therefore deprived Tehuti-nekht of all his offices and his property, and gave them to the *sekhti*, who thenceforth dwelt at the king's palace with all his family. And the *sekhti* became the chief overseer of Neb-ka-n-ra, and was greatly beloved by him.

STORY OF THE TWO BROTHERS

This tale, taken from a papyrus now in the British Museum, combines elements of folktale and mythology.

Anapou and Bitou were two brothers who lived in Egypt a long time ago. To Anapou, as the elder, belonged house, cattle, and fields; and Bitou, the younger, worked for him. Bitou was marvelously clever in his management of the cattle and in all things relating to agriculture – he could even tell what the cattle said to him and to each other.

One day, as the brothers were working in the fields, Anapou sent Bitou

A plan drawing from Tel el-Armana, showing a typical house with associated fields and granaries.

Egyptian cattle, near Denderah. Cattle were of great importance in the agriculture of Ancient Egypt, for use as draught animals as well as food.

The falcon-headed god Ra-Harmachis, a deity who incorporated aspects of the sun god Ra as well as Horus: he was also known as Horus of the Two Horizons, and represented the sun in daytime.

home for a large quantity of seed, as he saw the time had come for sowing. Bitou went and got the seed, but was approached with amorous intent by his brother's wife. He angrily rejected her advances and said nothing to his brother, but after their day's work the two returned, to find Anapou's wife lying moaning, and saying she had been thrashed by Bitou until she was sore because she would not yield herself to him when he came for the seed.

Then Anapou sought to kill Bitou by stealth, but Bitou, warned by the cattle, fled. His brother overtook him, but the god Ra-Harmachis caused a wide stream full of crocodiles to arise between them, and Bitou asked his brother to wait till break of day, when he would explain all that had happened.

When day broke Bitou told Anapou the truth, refusing at the same time ever to return to the house where Anapou's wife was. "I shall go," he said, "to the Vale of the Acacia. Now listen to what will happen. I shall tear out my heart by magic so as to place it on the topmost bough of the acacia, and when the acacia is cut down, and my heart will fall to the ground, you will come to look for it. After you have looked for seven years do not be discouraged, but put it in a vessel of cold water that will bring me to life again. I shall certainly live again and be revenged on my enemies. You will know that something of moment is about to happen to me when a jug of beer is given you and the froth shall run over. They will then give you a jug of wine of which the sediment will rise to the top. Rest no more when these things come about."

He went to the valley and his brother returned home, killed his wife, and mourned for Bitou. Bitou, in the valley, spent his days in hunting, and at night slept under the acacia, on top of which his heart was placed. One day he met the nine gods, who gave him the daughter of the gods for his wife; but the Seven Hathors swore she should die by the sword. He told her about his heart, and that whoever should find the acacia would have to fight with him.

The Apis-bull of Memphis was an ancient god, considered to be an incarnation of Osiris, with whom any sacrificial bull was associated. Apis is always shown with the solar disk between his horns.

The Treachery of Bitou's Wife

Pharaoh, hearing of this beautiful woman, desired to take possession of her, and sent armed men into the valley, all of whom Bitou killed. Pharaoh at last enticed her away and made her his chief favourite. She told him her husband's secret and bade him cut down the acacia-tree, which was accordingly done, and Bitou fell down dead at the same moment.

Then what Bitou had foretold happened to his brother. Beer that foamed was brought to him, and then wine which became muddy while he held the cup. By these signs he knew that the time had come to act, and taking his clothes and sandals and weapons, he set off for the valley. When he got there he found his brother lying dead on his bed. He went to the acacia to look for the heart, but could find only a berry, which, however, was the heart. He placed it in cold water, and Bitou was restored to life. They embraced each other, and Bitou said to his brother, "I shall now become a sacred bull (Apis). Lead me, then, to Pharaoh, who will reward you with gold and silver for having brought me. I shall then find means to punish my wife for having betrayed me."

Anapou did as Bitou directed, and when the sun rose again next day, Bitou having then assumed the form of a bull, he led him to court. There were great rejoicings over the miraculous bull, and Pharaoh rewarded Anapou richly and preferred him before any other man.

Some days after, the bull entered the harem and addressed his former wife.

"You see, I am still alive, after all," he said.

"Who are you?" she asked.

He said, "I am Bitou. You knew well what you were doing when you got Pharaoh to have the acacia cut down."

Then she was very much afraid, and begged Pharaoh to grant her any request she would make. Pharaoh, who loved her so much that he could refuse her nothing, consented. "Then," she said, "Give me the liver of the sacred bull to eat, for nothing else will satisfy me."

Pharaoh was very much grieved at this, but he had sworn, and one day when the people were offering up sacrifices to the bull he sent his butchers to cut its throat. When the bull was being killed two big drops of blood fell from his neck, and flowing till they were opposite Pharaoh's doorway, they sprang up in the form of two great trees, one at either side of the portal.

At this second miracle all the people rejoiced again and offered sacrifices to the two trees.

A long time after, Pharaoh, in his crown of lapis-lazuli, with a garland

A drawing of an Egyptian huntsman, returning home with the game on his shoulders and accompanied by his two hunting dogs.

A sacrificial bull being led, in a bas-relief from a temple at Luxor. Sacrifices were made to Apis in the form of offerings to the bull, before the animal itself was slaughtered.

of flowers round his neck, got into his electrum chair and was carried out to look at the two trees. His chief favourite – Bitou's wife – was brought after him and they were set down, one under each tree.

Then Bitou, from the tree under which his wife was seated, whispered to her, "Faithless woman! I am Bitou, and I am still alive in spite of you. You made Pharaoh cut down the acacia, and killed me. Then I became a bull and you had me slain."

The pharaoh Amenhotep III (opposite) seated on his throne and wearing the blue crown of lapis-lazuli, from a modern copy of an Egyptian painting.

An acacia bush, common in Egypt. The last incarnation of Bitou in the "Story of the Two Brothers" was as an acacia tree.

Afterward, when she was seated again with Pharaoh at table, she made him swear another oath to do whatever she asked him, and Pharaoh swore again. Then she said, "Cut me down these two trees and make them into two good beams."

What she demanded was done, but as the trees were being cut down a chip flew into her mouth. In due time she brought forth a male child, whom Pharaoh loved and made Prince of the Upper Nile, and when Pharaoh died, Bitou, for he was this child, succeeded him. Then he summoned all the great officials, had his wife brought before him, and told them all that had happened. So she was put to death.

Bitou lived and reigned for twenty years, and then his brother Anapou, whom he had made his successor, reigned in his stead.

THE STORY OF RHAMPSINITES

A common story in both Eastern and Western mythology, this tale was preserved in its Egyptianized form by Herodotus. It is impossible to account definitively for its origins.

King Rhampsinites possessed so much treasure that none of his successors ever surpassed or even came near to having a like amount. To ensure its safety he had a seemingly impregnable stone house built, in which he placed all his great wealth. By a clever trick, however, the architect contrived to provide access to the treasure. He made one of the stones in two parts, so that one part could be removed; but so skilfully were the two parts placed together that they presented a perfectly even surface, as of one single stone. Before he died he acquainted his two sons with the secret of the treasure-house, and after his death they did not delay in putting their knowledge into practice. They went by night, found the stone without any difficulty, withdrew it, stole a large sum of money, and replaced the two parts of the stone in position.

When the king discovered that thieves were at work he had man-traps placed near the site of the treasure-house. One night the two brothers came as usual, and one of them was caught in a trap. Seeing his danger, he called his brother and said to him, "We shall both perish and the treasure be lost unless you cut off my head and take it away, so that no one will recognize us as the thieves." The brother did as he advised: he moved the stone back into position, cut off his brother's head and carried it home.

When the king found the headless body he was much disturbed, for there were no traces of entrance to or exit from the treasure-house, and he bethought himself of this expedient: he had the dead body exposed on the city wall and placed a guard round it with instructions to watch and report whoever manifested any sign of grief on seeing the body. This act was contrary to the practice of the Egyptians, who had usually too much respect for the dead to indulge in it. Even in the case of an executed criminal the remains were returned to the relatives to be embalmed. Nevertheless Rhampsinites considered himself justified in adopting this measure.

The body was exposed, and the mother, although she did not betray any sign of grief, insisted on her other son bringing it to her; otherwise she threatened to divulge his secret to the king. Seeing that he dared not disobey, the son devised a stratagem. He saddled some asses and loaded them with goatskins full of wine – skins were used in Egypt for water only at most times, wine being held in short narrow vases – he drove the asses past the guard and, when passing, stealthily untied one or two of the skins, and as the wine ran down and flowed on the ground began to beat his head and make a great outcry.

The guards ran for vessels to save the precious liquid, and over the catastrophe they became quite friendly with the thief and gave him meat, for which he offered in exchange one of his skins of wine. They all sat down to drink together, and as they became merry over the wine he offered them the remainder of his wine, which they took and drank until they were quite tipsy.

The thief, needless to say, had taken care to remain tolerably sober. After the guards were in a drunken sleep, he waited till nightfall and then cut down his brother's body and took it home on the asses to his mother. Before quitting

The pharaohs of Egypt were the possessors of great wealth, including objects made from gold, acquired in quantity from mines near the Red Sea. Here part of a pharaoh's treasure is displayed at the museum in Cairo.

People throwing dust on their heads as a sign of grief following the death of a pharaoh.

the guards he shaved off all the hair on one side of their faces.

When the king heard of the trick he was furious, and, determined by fair means or foul to discover its author, he hit upon the following plan. He ordered the princess, his daughter, to receive any man in the land, no matter whom, and to grant him whatever favour he might ask of her, but first she must make him tell her what was the cleverest and wickedest thing he had ever done. When the thief told her his trick she was to have him bound before he could escape.

The princess was ready to do her father's bidding, but the thief, knowing well what the king had in his mind, resolved to circumvent him a third time. He cut off the arm of a newly dead man and, hiding it under his robe, obtained admission to the princess. On being asked the question that she put to all comers, he told her first about cutting off his brother's head in the trap, and then went on to tell how, having made the guards tipsy, he had cut down his brother's body.

She at once called out and tried to seize him, but he placed in her hand that of the dead man, which she grasped firmly, believing it to be the thief's, and he escaped in the darkness of the room.

The king now acknowledged himself beaten, and offered a free pardon and rich rewards to the man who had so boldly outwitted him. Trusting to his word, the thief presented himself before the king, and received not only what Rhampsinites had promised, but also the hand of the princess in marriage, for he held the thief to be the cleverest of men in that he had duped the Egyptians, who prided themselves on their astuteness.

A relief from Karnak showing four wine skins. Though beer was the most common alcoholic drink in Ancient Egypt, wine was also consumed in quantity by the aristocracy.

INDEX

INDEX

ACKNOWLEDGMENTS

James Putnam: 18, 72, 74-5, 89, 96, 100, 120, 123 (top), 138.

Spectrum Colour Library: 1, 2, 4, 6, 8, 9 (top), 10, 11 (top), 12, 14, 15 (bottom), 20 (top), 21, 25 (left), 27 (bottom), 30, 32 (bottom), 33 (top), 34, 36, 37, 39 (top), 42, 43, 44, 47 (top), 49 (bottom), 51 (bottom), 52 (top), 54, 55, 59 (top), 61, 63, 64, 68, 69, 70 (bottom), 71, 76, 78, 79 (left), 81 (top), 83 (bottom left), 84, 86, 87, 90, 91, 92, 93, 94, 102, 103, 104, 105, 106, 109 (top), 110, 111 (top and bottom), 113 (bottom), 114 (top), 117, 118, 126, 128, 131, 132, 133 (bottom), 135 (left), 137 (bottom), 139, 140 (top), 141.

Other illustrations are from:
The Ancient Egyptians – Their Life and Customs by Sir J. Gardner Wikinson
Panthéon Égyptien by M. J. Champollion
The Gods of the Egyptians and *Osiris and the Egyptian Resurrection* by E. A. Wallis Budge

The publishers have made every effort to locate and credit the copyright holders of material reproduced in this book, and regret any errors or omissions.